SECOND EDITION

THE ART OF
INQUIRY

Questioning Strategies
for K–6 Classrooms

Nancy Lee Cecil • Jeanne Pfeifer

PORTAGE & MAIN PRESS

Portage & Main Press gratefully acknowledges the financial support of the
Province of Manitoba through the Department of Culture, Heritage, Tourism &
Sport and the Manitoba Book Publishing Tax Credit and the Government of
Canada through the Canada Book Fund (CBF) for our publishing activities.

Printed and bound in Canada by Friesens
Cover and interior design by Relish Design Ltd.

Library and Archives Canada Cataloguing in Publication
Cecil, Nancy Lee

        The art of inquiry : questioning strategies for K-6 classrooms / Nancy Lee
Cecil and Jeanne Pfeifer. ~ 2nd ed.

Includes bibliographical references.
ISBN 978-1-55379-254-3

        1. Questioning. 2. Elementary school teaching.
3. Learning. I. Pfeifer, Jeanne II. Title.

LB1027.44.C43 2011   372.13   C2010-908045-9

PORTAGE & MAIN PRESS

100-318 McDermot Ave.
Winnipeg, MB Canada R3A 0A2
Email: books@portageandmainpress.com
Toll free: 1-800-667-9673
Fax free: 1-866-734-8477
www.pandmpress.com

To Landon and Katrina, who inspire me with their incessant questions and curiosity.

— N L C

To my parents, who encourage curiosity and questions — with compassion and integrity.

— J P

CONTENTS

PREFACE TO THE SECOND EDITION

Since the publication of *The Art of Inquiry* in 1995, educators have refined and elaborated on many of the questioning and inquiry strategies included in the book. In this edition, we have updated these strategies to reflect the changes. For example, some models recommended for narrative text have been adapted for information text. Some strategies include additional steps or new examples to help teachers and students better understand the purpose of an activity. Some strategies that were originally introduced at intermediate levels have been expanded and applied to primary grades.

This second edition also features several new strategies – including concept formation, concept attainment, and inductive reasoning. These strategies are intended to help students learn how to analyze data that lead to problem solving and decision making. We have also added new vignettes across the curriculum.

Many of the classroom examples in this edition take students beyond reading – to a place where they can reflect not only on structured activities but on their reading experiences.

Throughout this second edition, we have tried to differentiate between higher-level cognitive questioning and critical thinking. Higher-level cognitive questions help students think at more complex levels. Critical thinking encourages students to question what they are thinking so that they can improve the quality of their thinking.

We think you will agree that the changes and additions we have made to *The Art of Inquiry* reflect today's best practices in education.

ACKNOWLEDGMENTS

This book maintains that the art of questioning is a very exciting form of social interaction. In many ways, so too is writing a book about questioning. We must acknowledge the valuable interactions of the many colleagues and students who have shared their ideas and experiences with us during our years at California State University. These people are too numerous to mention by name, but their voices, spirit – even their work samples – are reflected throughout the book.

We would like to thank our editor, Leigh Hambly, for her considerable skill in bringing this book to print, for handling all the details, and for actually caring about the book as much as we do.

INTRODUCTION
to *The Art of Inquiry*

Why do people choose to become teachers? Having read, through the years, the professional goal statements of hundreds of eager students entering the field of education, we are amazed at how many mention "the excitement of seeing a light bulb go on inside a little head when the child suddenly understands a concept or an idea." Most present and future teachers, it seems, are attracted to the profession by the promise of those blissful moments when a child under their tutelage appears to have *learned*. Often, it is children's answers to questions about what they are reading or studying that are taken as the evidence that this learning has, indeed, taken place.

And that is the premise of this book: Asking elementary-age children just the right kinds of questions is directly related to these heady instances of sudden understanding. Throughout this second edition of *The Art of Inquiry*, pre-service and practicing teachers will discover numerous ideas about how to model provocative, open-ended questions and how to help young students learn to ask their own critical questions about content.

Our world has changed considerably since *The Art of Inquiry* was first published in 1995. Back then, students acquired most of their information from television, radio, and books. Students still get information from those media. Today, however, students are much more inclined to use computers, iPods, and cell phones to access the seemingly endless stream of information available on the Internet. Unfortunately, not all electronic information is valid, reliable, or even correct. Students must be able to evaluate the reliability of information they acquire.

The average life expectancy in North America in 1900 was just over 47 years. By 2010, the average life expectancy was beyond 80 years. Most of today's students are expected to live more than 60 years beyond the time they graduate from high school. Teachers, however, cannot teach their students everything they will need to know during their first 18 years. Nor do students learn everything they are taught in school. Beyond their school years, they will continue to learn. It is important, then, that students be taught inquiry and questioning strategies they can use for a lifetime of learning.

HOW TO USE THIS BOOK

We have divided this book into two sections. In Part I, we describe the taxonomy of questions, their uses, and the environmental factors necessary for the free flow of questions and answers in the classroom. We explore the types of questions that teachers can ask, and we present a definition, description, and an example of each type. A self-check is also included so that teachers can determine their own ability to identify the various levels of questions and, perhaps, begin asking more questions of a critical or open-ended nature.

Then, we focus on how to create the ideal environment for questioning – a classroom climate in which young learners feel free to ask and answer questions, where they feel competent to ask about topics that interest them, and where they can work with one another to investigate issues. We also include caveats about common practices that tend to squelch creative and critical thinking, thereby thwarting question asking and answering.

In Part II, we address specific questioning strategies that teachers can use to ask more thought-provoking questions, thus enhancing their students' construction of meaning from text and critical thinking. Next, we give suggestions and provide strategies that teachers can use to enable their students to generate their *own* questions. Then, we show how questioning strategies can be integrated across the entire curriculum, and we examine strategies particularly appropriate for math, science, social studies, and art appreciation.

Finally, for those teachers who are interested in reading more about questioning techniques and critical thinking, we have included an extensive bibliography of books, articles, and papers on these topics.

WHO THIS BOOK IS FOR

This book is for teachers of grades K–6 who are already convinced magic can occur when they ask just the right kinds of questions. Such teachers want to develop their questioning skills to a level where their students are noticeably more involved in the learning process. This book is also for all pre-service teachers who still fantasize about the joy they will experience when they see *the light bulb go on*. When teachers ask the right questions of their students, they stimulate in-depth thinking and invite sudden connections and insights. It is in the classrooms of such teachers that light bulbs can be observed going on in young heads – all day long.

PART I
The Importance of Good Questions

Just how important are questions in the academic life of a child? According to Rubin (2009), well-fashioned, intentional questions give students opportunities to connect different aspects of content and, thus, develop deep understandings that they can transfer across content. Sigel and Saunders (1979) say that questioning is critical, because it requires children to distance themselves in time and space from the present. Sigel (1982, 50) defines distancing as the "psychological separation of [the student] from the immediate, ongoing present." When responding to questions about past or future events, the child shifts from the present to another, distant, mode of thought, rather than simply responding to current observable events. Thinking about past or future events requires an abstract mental representation of what has happened or of what may soon happen. The ability to abstract calls for a higher plane of thinking that results, ultimately, in increased learning (Rosenshine, Meister, and Chapan 1996).

Asking questions also appears to be an effective way to direct and develop reading comprehension in children, especially when the teacher models good questions and shows children how to ask their own questions. Asking one's own questions is a form of making predictions and is essential to comprehension – it forces one to construct meaning rather than passively accept text as it is encountered. Children who are good predictors – and, therefore, good self-questioners – are also good comprehenders of text (Kestler 1992; Ouzts 1998; Jones and Leahy 2006).

Finally, imagination can be enhanced only when children are given the opportunity to play with ideas, to discover relationships, and, most important, to ask questions. Educators who show children that their ideas have value and their questions will be carefully considered add a rich source of fuel to children's motivation for learning. Children who are encouraged to ask and answer carefully crafted questions are being given opportunities to explore with their minds, to gain meaning for themselves, and to relate new data to old ideas. And when children seek to ask or answer questions about things or events for which there is no one right answer (or for which there are many potentially correct answers), they begin to develop an attitude of appreciation for the immensity and complexity of the natural world (Barell 2003). This is when true learning begins to take place within and beyond the classroom doors!

WHAT ARE THE RIGHT QUESTIONS?

Most teachers believe that asking students questions facilitates the learning and cognitive development of learners. It is not surprising, therefore, that over 50 percent of adult verbal interactions with young children are composed of adult questions (Blank and Allen 1976). Studies involving elementary-school teachers reveal that they ask their students about 3.5 questions per minute, with teachers asking approximately 27 questions for every student question (Floyd 1960). To improve the quality of the questions teachers ask, it helps to examine the types of questions asked, their impact on students' learning, and the teacher's role in facilitating that learning. From this information, helpful strategies and techniques for asking questions can be developed.

Research on questioning suggests that teachers are not asking enough of the kinds of open-ended questions that enhance a child's imagination and facilitate critical thinking. Bromley (1992, 139) draws the following conclusions:

- Seventy-five percent of the questions teachers ask are of a factual or a literal nature.
- Over 50 percent of the questions contained in the basal readers, still pervasively used in elementary schools, are of a factual or a literal nature.
- Teachers ask an average of 70 factual or literal questions in an average 30-minute lesson.

Over the last few years, the importance of reading and math as separate subjects has been emphasized. This emphasis is often to the exclusion of social studies, science, the arts, physical education, and to the integration of these subject areas. Children do not normally encounter situations in life from a single discipline area. To successfully solve problems, students must be able to call upon multiple areas of study. One major purpose of inquiry and problem-based learning involves students in real-world problems, asking authentic questions, gathering data leading to decision making, problem solving, logical thinking, or creative thinking (Presseisen 2001).

Costa (2001) reminds us that children have a universal, inquisitive nature, and that they are continually asking questions to learn or to challenge ideas. However, he argues, without the open-ended *why* questions, the *whats* and the *hows* that generally precede factual questions will not really matter very much to children. Neither the question nor the answer will draw the child in, or engage his or her mind in a meaningful way. The *why* questions, Costa (2001, 246) avows, are critical because they jump to "...the core of our curriculum [to] focus on such processes as learning to learn, knowledge production, metacognition, transference, decision making, creativity and group problem solving."

THE LIMITATIONS OF FACTUAL QUESTIONS

Why do most teachers ask so many factual questions? Teachers may believe that factual questions are easier to answer, because only small amounts of specific information are needed to answer them. But this is not so. A child with good critical-thinking skills may know all about Columbus's difficulties securing support for his explorations from Italian, Spanish, and Portuguese royalty, but be unable to remember the exact year Columbus sailed to America. Teachers may also believe there are fewer possible answers to dispute with factual questions than there are with interpretive or evaluative questions (which often involve background knowledge or personal opinion). But by responding only to factual questions, students miss out on the critical – and creative – thinking benefits that derive from rigorous discussion. Some teachers believe that students must know a certain number of facts before they can think critically. The problem with this assumption is that students may never know enough facts, so the teacher and students never get around to critical thinking. Critical thinking can occur while students are learning facts and new content and may even direct them toward new information. Finally, some teachers may emphasize factual questions, because such questions require concise answers. Teachers may think that classroom behavior can be more easily controlled when many students are involved in fast-paced questioning and answering. If this is the case, the teacher is inviting students to become superficially involved in an *inquisition*, but never actively engaged in *inquiry*.

What subtle messages do teachers who ask mainly factual questions give their students? Children may get the impression that facts and details are more important than personal interpretations or evaluations of events and ideas. They may feel they are not intelligent if they happen to have short-term memories and ignore names and dates in favor of, for example, more global, schematic impressions. Moreover, in classrooms where factual answers are emphasized, children often get little opportunity to use oral language to elaborate their ideas or to talk in-depth about meaningful content. Instead, they too often spend their time answering factual questions in monosyllables, or filling in blanks on worksheets in the same, uninspired manner. Students are less likely to remember facts when they do not use the information in meaningful ways. Students who engage in problem-based learning use higher-order questions; they acquire not only factual information but also information-processing skills.

CHAPTER 1
The Question of Questions

Most educators agree that one of the major goals of teaching is to help children learn to make reasoned decisions in life. To do so, children must be taught to actively solve problems, to think critically and creatively, and to feel good about themselves. Trilling and Fadel (2009) list these as essential skills for the 21st century. Children acquire these necessary thinking skills by learning to form and respond to critical questions. Teachers may help children accomplish these goals within a required curriculum of knowledge acquisition, or, in sharp contrast, they may simply fill the minds of children with a series of unrelated facts as if their minds were empty vessels.

Learning to ask appropriate questions is a sophisticated art form, but it is an area that receives short shrift in most teacher-education programs. This is unfortunate. Research indicates that teachers specifically trained to ask high-quality questions show significant improvement in constructing and using such questions in the classroom (Angletti 1991; Blanchard, Southerland, and Grandger 2008) and so become more adept at stimulating the human potential of their students. As well, being aware of the classification of questions and their myriad forms helps teachers determine just how well they are doing at engaging their students in critical and creative thinking levels.

Questioning is effective for so many purposes that teachers must be skilled in its use. They need to know the many ways of asking, and how to adapt the type and form of each question to the purpose for which it is asked. Because questioning is so important, this entire chapter is devoted to helping the teacher become familiar with the different levels of questions in both the cognitive and the affective domains.

PURPOSE OF QUESTIONS

Teachers use questions in the classroom for many different purposes (see figure 1.1). Often, these purposes work simultaneously. For instance, a teacher might ask a question to test students' understandings of a specific concept while, at the same time, ask students to use the concept to make a decision or solve a problem. The teacher may also ask the question to elicit an attitude or feeling about a topic.

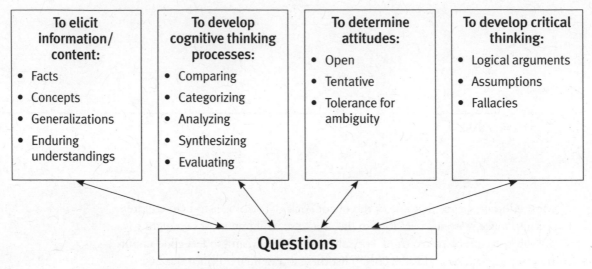

To elicit information/content:
- Facts
- Concepts
- Generalizations
- Enduring understandings

To develop cognitive thinking processes:
- Comparing
- Categorizing
- Analyzing
- Synthesizing
- Evaluating

To determine attitudes:
- Open
- Tentative
- Tolerance for ambiguity

To develop critical thinking:
- Logical arguments
- Assumptions
- Fallacies

Questions

Figure 1.1 This chart shows the multiple purposes of questions.

TYPES OF QUESTIONS

The Cognitive Domain

The basic framework for the types of questions used in most classrooms comes from the work of Bloom. In his book *Taxonomy of Educational Objectives*, Bloom (1984) presents six major cognitive – or thinking – operations: knowledge, comprehension, application, analysis, synthesis, and evaluation.

Bloom's six types of questions can be grouped into three larger categories according to the level of processing that is required of students who are answering them (see figure 1.2). Level I questions – knowledge and comprehension – are lower-level questions. They require children to gather and recall data, but call for minimal complex thinking. Level I questions are designed mainly to solicit from students concepts, information, feelings, or experiences that have been gathered in the past and stored in the memory. Level II questions – application and analysis – ask the students to begin to process data and to integrate new content with their own experiences. Level III questions – synthesis and evaluation – are called higher-level questions. They require a high level of mental operation. To answer, students must engage in more abstract and sophisticated thinking that requires them to evaluate data in an entirely new situation, or to predict future events. At this level, questions are designed to encourage students to think intuitively, creatively, and hypothetically, to use their imaginations, to reveal their value systems, or to make judgments.

Level	Question Type	Response Behaviors	Eliciting Question Starters
I	Knowledge	Recalling facts or observations. Recalling definitions.	1. Who...? 2. What...? 3. Where...? 4. When...? 5. Define (the word *prosper*).
	Comprehension	Giving descriptions.	1. Describe (what happened when the third goat went over the bridge). 2. What is the main idea (in this paragraph)? 3. How are (these two fruits alike)?
II	Application	Applying techniques.	1. If...then.... 2. What (is the perimeter of your living room)?
	Analysis	Identifying motives or causes. Making inferences. Finding evidence to support generalizations.	1. Why (did Old Yeller die)? 2. Now that we have studied whales, what can we conclude about zoos? (assumptions) 3. What evidence can you find to support (the point of view that students should not receive grades)?
III	Synthesis	Solving problems. Making predictions. Producing original communications.	1. Can you think of (a way to test this)? 2. How can we solve (this problem)? 3. How can we improve (our research)? 4. What will happen (now that we have found a cure for cancer)? 5. What do you predict would happen (if we all looked the same)?
	Evaluation	Giving opinions about issues. Judging the validity of ideas. Judging the merit of problem solutions. Judging the quality of art and other products. Judging opinions and ideas.	1. Do you agree (with José)? 2. Do you believe (that this is the best way to proceed)? Why? 3. Do you think (that it is right to judge criminals)? Why? 4. What is your opinion (on this matter)? Why? 5. Would it be better (to do it this way)? Why? 6. Which (video) did you like? Why?

Figure 1.2 This chart shows the types of questions in the cognitive domain.

Beyond Bloom's Taxonomy

Bloom's Taxonomy of cognitive objectives was published in the 1950s and has had an important influence on educators. Since that time, his work has been looked at through multiple lenses and elaborated upon by many. Not only have cognitive psychologists used the taxonomy to describe complex thinking but so too have philosophers, educators, and others in disciplines such as the sciences, social sciences, and the arts. A study group of teachers and university professors examined the thinking processes from a variety of fields and over several years evolved the following graphic organizer (see figure 1.3). This elaborate chart helps to pinpoint some of the steps that are necessary to engage students in problem solving or decision making. The chart helps to describe different purposes for complex processing of information. *Input* refers to the different types of knowledge. *Comparing, categorizing, sequencing,* and *point of view* elaborate on comprehension and application. *Problem solving, decision making, logical thinking,* and *creative thinking* expand on why we engage in analysis, synthesis, and evaluation.

When students are asked to research information, they need a place to organize it. The thinking processes they have used will not be meaningful if they are not aware of the purpose or questions they are pursuing.

Students become engaged in higher-order thinking for different purposes. They may need to solve a problem, make a decision, or find a solution to a logical dilemma usually too complex and messy without apparent answers at the beginning. Students must have some way of organizing and sorting the raw data, to be able to "make sense" of information and apply it to some end purpose.

THINKING PROCESSES			
Purpose or Question			
Input	**Elaboration**		**Output**
Primary Sources (first person): • Documents • Interviews • Surveys • Experimentation	Comparing Categorizing Hypothesizing	Analysis (whole to parts) Synthesis (parts creating a new whole)	Problem Solving Decision Making
Secondary Sources (someone else's interpretations): • Documents • Interviews • Surveys • Experimentation **Facts**	Sequencing Point of View	Evaluation (criteria applied to examples)	Logical Thinking Creative Thinking

© 2011 Pfeifer

Figure 1.3 This chart, useful for data collection and analysis, elaborates on Bloom's Taxonomy.

CRITICAL THINKING APPLIED TO THINKING PROCESSES			
SIMPLE			**COMPLEX**
Input	Elaboration		Output
Data/facts/resources: • Are they credible? • Does the person have the expertise? • Do the sources fit the problem/dilemma/situation? • Are the sources valid? • Are the sources representative of the population? • To whom might the data be generalized? • Are the data sufficient? • Is there bias?	Are *comparisons* complete, including necessary elements? Are *categories* complete? Have all relevant *points of view* been considered? Do patterns fit sparse data for *hypotheses*? Will more data be collected to confirm or deny hypotheses? Does language indicate tentativeness of *interpretation*? Does the order of *sequences* have support?	**Analysis:** Are all of the parts accounted for and explain or relate to the whole? Are relationships explained and credible? **Synthesis:** How has creativity been determined? Beyond odd, unusual? **Evaluation:** Are criteria evident? Relevant to the example(s)? Complete sets of criteria? Match the complexity of the task?	**Problem Solving:** Are objective criteria evident? Multiple alternatives considered? Generalizable? **Decision Making:** Major and sufficient alternatives considered? Values clear? Pros and cons consistent with values? **Logical:** Clear premises? Logical connections between premises? Avoid fallacies? **Creativity:** New, fresh, unique aspects? Combines things to create new outcomes?

Figure 1.4 The sample questions illustrate moving beyond thinking processes that lead to critical thinking.

Critical Thinking and Thinking Processes

Although critical thinking and thinking processes are similar to each other, they are not exactly the same. Bloom and his colleagues described a hierarchy of cognitive thinking processes; how the human mind processes information to remember, apply, and invent new information. Critical thinking is thinking about one's thinking to improve thinking (Paul and Elder 2006, 87). Critical thinking involves the *quality* of thinking. Students are asked to apply nine standards of thinking to their own claims as well as to the claims of others. These standards include the consideration of clarity, accuracy, precision, relevance, depth, breadth, logicalness, significance, and fairness. As students collect information there are a number of questions they can ask themselves (see figure 1.4).

As teachers design lessons to engage students in inquiry, they must pay attention to not only the cognitive (brain) processes, but also to how attitudes, values, beliefs, and feelings impact ideas – the affective domain.

The Affective Domain

Bloom also considered questions in the affective domain – questions that deal mainly with feelings and emotions. In reality, the cognitive and affective domains cannot be separated, for it is almost impossible for children, or for anyone else, to process information without some emotional response. Nor can they actually value an issue without having thought about it. It seems that both domains tend to blend and flow concurrently. However, certain questions may be more relevant to one domain than to the other.

The five types of questions in the affective domain are: receiving, responding, valuing, organizing, and characterizing. These can be grouped according to the level of processing required (see figure 1.5), as are the cognitive domain questions. Receiving and responding are considered Level I, or lower-level questions. While both require that a child be somewhat involved in the activity or idea, there is little real commitment in his or her answer. Level II questions – valuing – require students to "think harder" and, thus, to commit themselves to the degree that the resulting behavior is consistent and stable enough to be called a belief or an attitude. Level III questions, or higher-level questions, involve organizing and

Level	Question Type	Response Behaviors	Eliciting Question Starters
I	Receiving (attending)	Awareness of environment. Willingness to receive.	1. Which would you prefer…? 2. Identify the person who…. 3. Listen to this song by…. 4. Are you aware that…?
	Responding	Acquiescence in responding. Willingness to respond. Satisfaction in response.	1. Do you like to sing? 2. Did you observe the difference between the two pieces? 3. Are you willing to go to the ballet?
II	Valuing	Acceptance of a value. Preference for a value. Commitment.	1. Defend your stance (on gun control). 2. Do you feel (responsible for the homeless)? 3. Rank order your preferences…. 4. Do you agree or disagree that…?
III	Organization	Conceptualization of a value. Organization of a value system.	1. In your opinion (is this money well spent)? 2. As you view (the war, should we have entered the conflict)? 3. In your own words, explain the issue. 4. Have you weighed the alternatives (for not using animal research)?
	Characterization	Generalized set. A philosophy of life. Values are internalized.	1. What will you do (about pollution)? 2. Are you willing to (give up lunch one day a week for the homeless)? 3. What is your philosophy (on mercy killings)? 4. Which of the following beliefs would you say is the most important in your life?

Figure 1.5 This chart shows the types of questions in the affective domain.

characterizing. Such questions are successful when they provoke the students to internalize their values, act upon those values, or organize them into a consistent value system that they are willing to defend.

Affective-type questions that represent all levels should be present in all class discussions, although not all levels need to be used in every lesson. The skilled teacher devises cognitive questions to stimulate students to process information with the final goal of analyzing data and evaluating it. That same teacher uses affective questions to elicit feeling-laden responses from students, and invites them to develop a value system that will become part of their daily lives.

Many educators suggest that certain dispositions, attitudes, values, and feelings enhance a learner's opportunities to solve problems, make decisions, and think critically. These include, for example, being open minded, respecting others' points of view, respecting evidence, being a risk taker, being objective, being a perfectionist, having the ability to stay focused on the main issue, having perseverance, and having healthy skepticism (questioning).

Other Types of Questions

Higher-order questions elicit multiple, high-level responses. If, however, students provide partial or narrow responses, the teacher may ask questions that invite students to think about the question in different ways. In addition to Bloom's two taxonomies, Costa (1991, 2001) identifies several other ways of looking at the questions teachers ask in classrooms to elicit desired responses: clarifying, cuing, focusing, and probing.

- Clarifying questions. When the teacher does not understand what the student is saying or hopes to get the student to elaborate, clarifying questions can be asked. Examples include: Are you saying that gang members provide the same function as parents? Would you tell us more about why you think that is so, and give an example of what you are thinking?

- Cuing questions. Often a teacher asks a leading question to launch a lesson – only to be greeted by total silence, because the students lack the background information to answer the question. In these instances, the teacher provides hints in the form of questions. For example, the teacher might initially ask: Why do you think so many people went westward in the pioneer days? When greeted with silence, the teacher tries cuing, What effect did the discovery of gold in California have on the settlers' decision to go west? or What discovery in California caused great excitement?

- Focusing questions. A teacher asks a focusing question when directing the learners' attention to a particular issue or topic. A teacher might ask, for example: Should there be a leash law in Sacramento? Then, the teacher can begin to elicit opinions and draw the whole class into a discussion on the pros and cons of the issue.

- Probing questions. Without the follow-up of probing questions, many important questions receive simple responses. For example, the teacher asks: Should we have sent troops to Afghanistan? A student answers, Absolutely not! The teacher has an answer to the critical question, but no reasoned decision. The teacher may ask for an elaboration, more information, a reason, or a description of what the student is thinking: Why do you think that? By asking a probing question, the teacher can discover the depth of the student's thinking on the subject.

The Pervasive Initiate-Respond-Evaluate

A final word about questions concerns not the design of the questions themselves, but how the responses are evaluated by the questioner. For critical and creative thinking to flourish in a classroom, students must be free to respond to questions from their own trajectory of experiences, attitudes, and values. Unfortunately, in most classrooms, discussions follow the time-honored Initiate-Respond-Evaluate (IRE) pattern of question and answer (Roller 1989).

Using the IRE pattern, the teacher asks a question designed to get students ready to interact with what they are about to read. The teacher tries to connect what the students already know about a subject so that they will be more likely to assimilate new information easily. For example, prior to reading a story about a youngster who has won a prestigious award, the teacher initiates discussion by asking if anyone in the class has ever won an award. A student says her father once won an award in a refugee camp, for touching his nose with his tongue. Very quickly, almost subconsciously, the teacher evaluates and decides the response does not meet her expectation; it is not the academic-type award she has in mind. The child who answered the question has been unintentionally rebuked. From this, she learns she must try to figure out the answer that the teacher has in mind. Or, perhaps, she learns that it is safer to not respond at all (Cecil 1990).

Teachers who use IRE have a hidden agenda in asking the question. They control the interchange, subtly, by insisting all learners match their level of language, experience, and values. These teachers may continue to ask students for responses to a particular question until they get the answer they want. The questioning patterns used usually focus on fact/recall questions, the lowest levels of Bloom's Taxonomy. Such questions may limit students' use and application of information.

USING THE TAXONOMY OF QUESTIONS

The taxonomy of the types of questions just explored offers a variety of interesting possibilities related to teaching and learning. These possibilities are presented in random order, as individual differences in teachers and classrooms of students have a significant influence on the usability and success of a particular approach to questioning techniques. The following are ways in which awareness of types of questions could impact various curricular components:

- Building questions from reading material. Knowing the breadth of possibilities in both the cognitive and affective domains helps teachers create questions that build on one another hierarchically. Also, awareness of several models, descriptions, and verb delineations helps teachers develop questions that focus on particular cognitive skills or affective responses (see figure 1.6).

Providing opportunities for students to collect and interpret data. While it is important for students to become proficient readers, they also need opportunities to obtain information through a multitude of sources, and to solve real problems and experience "mucking around" as they sort through information and make sense of it. These opportunities often involve

---

Name: __Theo__   Date: __April 3__

Theme: __Martin Luther King, Jr.:The Life of a Great Man__

Question Type 1. Choose from the following verbs:

define	describe	observe
list	match	notice
identify	locate	

Student: I will describe the early life of Martin Luther King, Jr.

Question Type 2. Choose from the following verbs:

explain	rewrite	summarize
convert	interpret	give examples
paraphrase	respond	

Student: I will paraphrase Martin Luther King, Jr.'s "I Have a Dream" speech.

Question Type 3. Choose from the following verbs:

demonstrate	show	support an opinion
construct	operate	apply

Student: I will support my opinion that Dr. King was a "Great Man" by showing the many ways he changed life for Black Americans.

Question Type 4. Choose from the following verbs:

organize	deduct	value
infer	compare	analyze
contrast	categorize	distinguish

Student: I will compare the life of Dr. Martin Luther King, Jr. to that of Mahatma Gandhi.

Question Type 5. Choose from the following verbs:

create	design	suppose	compose
support	rearrange	combine	

Student: I will create my own "I Have a Dream" speech, including all the goals Dr. King had that have not yet been realized.

Question Type 6. Choose from the following verbs:

judge	debate	characterize	support
appraise	criticize	evaluate	

Student: I will write an essay in support of passive resistance and how it could end the violence in North American cities.

Figure 1.6 Students can be taught to use the taxonomy.

"hands-on learning." Teachers need to ensure that hands-on learning is also minds-on learning.

- Selecting curricula. When selecting different learning activities across the curricula, the overall objectives can be tied to reinforcing particular thinking skills or affective responses. This criterion for selection allows the teacher, as key decision maker, to choose activities with clear, broad-based instructional goals.

- Purchasing instructional materials. The taxonomy of questions can be used as a guideline for evaluating whether or not instructional materials tap the full range of thinking and valuing levels, as opposed to specific content matter. Materials may include primary sources, supplemental text materials, and visual aids such as software and Internet sources.

- Teaching the taxonomy to students. Students can be taught to use the taxonomy by having them select from a series of options that cover the entire range of thinking processes. To do this, have students choose an issue, theme, or problem. Then, using question types, they select verbs from each level of the taxonomy as a way to explore the topic (see figure 1.6). Finally, from the top rung of either the cognitive or affective taxonomy, they select a means for displaying a product of their exploration. In the affective domain, for example, an exploration of capital punishment might lead to a final product of a letter to the government representative stating the student's argument for or against. In the cognitive domain, an essay might be the vehicle through which the student evaluates the relative validity of passive resistance by exploring the life of Mahatma Gandhi or Martin Luther King, Jr.

- Independent study. Many teachers are uncomfortable with student independent study, because they must evaluate an "orphan" product – that is, they cannot measure it against the work of other students to help establish a norm. But in independent study, higher-level thinking skills are experienced by the learner in a natural way. Using the taxonomy as a criterion, the teacher can analyze the range of thinking (or valuing) within the student's activities.

- Small-group study. When students work together, they learn important social skills; they are also motivated by what and by how other students think. Additionally, responses to some questions are so long that a student does not have enough time to answer them. In small groups, students can divide such questions into parts, with each student being responsible for one part. The group can then teach the rest of the class what each student learned.

- Assessing verbal interactions. Teachers know intuitively that classroom discussions provide students with meaningful forums for oral-language development, intellectual experiences, and discovering values. However, in this age of accountability, evaluating these discussions may be difficult. At various times throughout the school year, the use of portfolios and authentic assessments enables teachers to keep informal anecdotal records of the quality and types of questions initiated by each student during discussions.

The above suggestions represent several possible uses for the cognitive and affective questioning taxonomies. While their usefulness will vary according to different teaching styles and situations, they do provide structure and a viable rationale for the curriculum selection process. If used appropriately and integrated throughout the curriculum, the taxonomies and other types of questions can offer welcome guidelines for teachers wishing to boost the level of cognitive and affective functioning in their classrooms.

AN EXERCISE FOR IDENTIFYING TYPES AND LEVELS OF QUESTIONS

The exercise in figure 1.7 assesses your recognition and understanding of the types (cognitive or affective) and levels (I, II, or III) of questions that we have discussed in this chapter. Mark each question with a letter (C for cognitive or A for affective) and a number corresponding to the level (I, II, or III). In many cases, a question can contain elements of both domains or, depending on the actual response, straddle two different levels. For this exercise, however, mark the type and level that best fits the question.

IDENTIFYING TYPES AND LEVELS OF QUESTIONS

_____ 1. Do you recall the difference between a camel and a dromedary?

_____ 2. What is your reaction to the position Mr. Potter has taken regarding the leash law in Sacramento?

_____ 3. Explain how the habitats of the two turtles are similar. How are they different?

_____ 4. Which of the poems do you think was the most interesting?

_____ 5. If you were offered a trip to China this summer, how would you react?

_____ 6. Compose an essay that would tell about your outlook on school.

_____ 7. What is the capital of Illinois?

_____ 8. Indicate your reaction to the man who says he loves nature but who goes deer hunting.

_____ 9. How do you feel about reading?

_____ 10. How might these geometric shapes be grouped?

_____ 11. What do you think will happen when Jud finds out the boy has Shiloh?

_____ 12. How does life today differ from life in the times of the pioneers?

_____ 13. Write a short essay relating how you interpret the role of government with regard to providing housing for the homeless.

_____ 14. Indicate philosophically how you feel about the death penalty.

_____ 15. What do you think transportation will be like in the year 2525?

_____ 16. What do you think will be the long-term effect of pollution if nothing is done to stop it?

_____ 17. What do you think caused Jesse to change his mind about Leslie?

_____ 18. Do all trees have leaves?

_____ 19. Is there any type of activity you would like to try over any other?

Answers:

1. C,I   2. A,II   3. C,I   4. A,II   5. A,II   6. A,III   7. C,I   8. A,I   9. A,II   10. C,II   11. C,III   12. C,II   13. C,III   14. A,III   15. C,III   16. C,III   17. C,II   18. C,II   19. A,II

Figure 1.7 Assessment excercise

CHAPTER 2
The Ideal Climate for Questioning

The climate in many North American classrooms inhibits students from asking and answering questions. In such classrooms, silence and order are the most important features, and strict adherence to teacher-imposed rules is dutifully enforced. The atmosphere can be described as chilly, and the brains of learners have great difficulty warming up. Students' spirits shrink, and their little bodies droop. Their minds do not grow; they contract. Students feel self-conscious about expressing themselves and are, therefore, never totally engaged in learning.

Fortunately, in many other classrooms children's faces are alive with excitement, and every hand is raised, because every child's imagination is churning and producing ideas. Young minds are being stimulated and challenged. The moment an observer enters one of these classrooms, he or she notices how questions and answers abound, often initiated by the students themselves. Classrooms that contain this kind of enthusiastic intellectual interchange strengthen the spirits of students and spark the flames of curiosity and self-worth (Clyde and Hicks 2008). The students are proud of their work, respectful of their own ideas and the ideas of others, and welcome new experiences. Such classrooms reflect Ashton-Warner's observation that "energy and curiosity make good desk-mates" (1974, 117). Consumer advocate and former presidential candidate Ralph Nader remembers his father asking him what he learned in school one day. Did he learn how to believe or did he learn how to think? (Nader 2006). We can only hope that students learn to think.

In this chapter, we examine the classroom that is filled with enthusiasm. It is the kind of classroom that is most conducive to encouraging students to ask and answer questions reflectively and honestly. We also explore common practices to avoid, because they tend to squelch open and thoughtful behavior.

REMOVING BLOCKS TO CRITICAL THINKING

One way to develop the willingness and the ability to ask and answer critical and creative questions is to remove factors that block the free flow of the production of ideas. In some cases, the teacher must try to undo patterns of passive behavior that have been established in previous teacher-dominated classrooms. In other cases, the teacher may need to provide children with a necessary knowledge base from which they can begin to ask and answer reflective questions.

Knowledge

Before students can ask and answer reflective questions, they must have some basis of factual awareness of the topic or problem under investigation. In other words, they cannot examine the topic critically or offer creative solutions or observations if they know nothing about the subject. For example, a teacher may launch a unit on rain forests by asking a high-level, critical-thinking question such as, Why are rain forests important to us? This may be a good, essential question to make students curious and interested. However, it is a poor first question if the teacher expects the students to give a response at the beginning of the unit of study. Many students may not know enough about the issues inherent in the question to offer a wide range of cogent responses. After defining rain forests and researching the effects of forests on our oxygen supply, exploring how wood is used in our daily lives, and discussing the pros and cons of deforestation, students are much more able and eager to respond to the original question, backing up their ideas, beliefs, and opinions with facts. Many skills are required before thoughtful, reasoned questions can be asked and answered, but acquiring the necessary knowledge base is an important first step in the total process. Of course, the essential question may be revisited throughout the lesson, and students can add information to the response as they learn more about rain forests.

Habits

Habit is another block to a free flow of questions and answers in the classroom. Certainly, it is human nature to get comfortable with a particular way of doing things, and the same is true with the asking and answering of questions. An example of this is when teachers ask all the questions (especially as indicated in the teacher's manual), instead of allowing students to ask their own questions and to answer one another's questions. While teachers may support the idea of a child-centered classroom in theory, many find themselves unable to break the habit of being the one controlling the discussion. Another habit common to teachers is same-line questioning, used in the same way, to all groups of learners, without considering the size of the group, the ability levels, the language proficiency, and so on.

Even without considering the unique qualities of the students, it is still true that a variety of question-and-answer techniques enhances the intellectual climate of the classroom. Teachers should take a long, hard look at their own habits to determine if they need to free themselves from entrenched questioning habits. They can keep a seating chart to record which students they tend to call upon.

They can number the questions to help them keep track of the sequence. Teachers can also ask themselves the following questions:

- Do I call on both boys and girls in representative numbers?
- Do I call on both "high" achievers and "low" achievers?
- Do I call equally on students who sit at the front of the room and students who sit at the back of the room?

Young students, too, develop habits that are hard to break. Due to a variety of cultural and personality factors, they may establish passive stances, and they often require special encouragement by a caring teacher to change from passive listeners to active participants in question-and-answer exchanges. Sometimes, students just do not answer, and there is a deafening silence. They may have learned, if they are quiet, that the teacher will eventually answer the question. While this lets them off the hook, they are not processing information and developing deep understandings. There are several strategies that teachers can use to help students participate, including the following:

- As a class, brainstorm ideas about the topic.
- Have students discuss the question with one or two classmates.
- Gently prompt students who know the answer.
- Encourage students by explaining that they do not have to know the complete answer: Everyone knows something; no one knows everything.

Attitudes

The final block to a free-flow production of questions and answers in the classroom is negativity. Over time, both teachers and students can develop this kind of attitude. A terse response such as, *That will never work!* to any new idea (for example, a change away from a teacher-centered classroom toward a child-centered classroom) is counterproductive. So, too, is an abrupt move to asking very young children high-level questions rather than just factual ones. Teachers must actively attempt to alter these negative attitudes so that, It can't work! becomes, Maybe I'll try and see!

Authority – who is in charge – is another problem. Teachers who see themselves as the ultimate authority in their classrooms often have a difficult time dealing with open-ended questions for which they may not have all the answers. These teachers are not usually comfortable allowing students to lead the discussion.

Teachers must also concern themselves with their students' attitudes toward authority. Many children are passive in the classroom, expect the teacher to have all the answers, and feel confused when they are asked to offer a viewpoint that may differ from the teacher's. Such children need to be invited to initiate questions concerning their own interests in the more accepting atmosphere of a student-centered classroom.

FACILITATING THE FREE FLOW OF PRODUCTION

As we have discussed, the teacher's goal is to help the students learn how to solve problems, make decisions, think critically and creatively, and feel good about themselves and their learning. How the teacher constructs questions and carries out questioning strategies has everything to do with the realization of these goals. In the remainder of this chapter, we look at how to prepare and implement the kinds of questions that arouse student interest and encourage their participation.

Careful Planning of Questions

Thorough preparation helps ensure that questions are clear and specific to students, the vocabulary is appropriate for the targeted learners, and each question matches its purpose. Questions should be incorporated into all lessons as effective instructional devices, welcomed pauses for reflection, attention grabbers, and viable checks for student comprehension.

For units and learning centers, one driving investigative question should be created to connect all the activities into a meaningful whole. For example, the question, Why did the pioneers go westward?, allows the teacher and students to focus on answering this one pivotal question throughout the rest of the unit. With a clear focus in mind, the teacher is less likely to include frivolous activities about pioneers – activities that may be fun for students but that do not add significantly to the body of knowledge being developed. Similarly, if students are aware of the overall investigative question, their responses to oral and written questions are much more likely to remain focused on the topic, and they can more easily understand how the activity is connected to other activities in the unit or learning center.

Additionally, when planning open-ended critical or creative questions, teachers must guard against having in mind preconceived answers that reflect their personal world views, values, and/or culture. They can best accomplish this by asking themselves the following:

- Do I have an answer for this question already in mind?
- Does the answer I am looking for reflect my personal belief system?
- Will I be open to a variety of thoughtful answers that do not match the one(s) that I have developed?

Matching Questions With Their Purposes

Carefully planned questions can be sequenced and worded to match the appropriate level of cognitive and affective thinking. To help students develop more effective thinking skills, the teacher must create questions that are easily understood and that students can relate to their own experiences. Constant modeling of the appropriate cognitive or affective terminology helps students focus their thinking in specific ways. Figure 2.1 provides examples of good, specifically worded questions in the left-hand column and poor, vaguely worded questions in the right-hand column.

QUESTION COMPARISON	
Specific Question	**Vague Question**
• What evidence do you have to support your ideas about that?	• How do you know that?
• What does that music remind you of in your own life?	• Do you like that music?
• How would you apply that concept to your own budgeting?	• What did you learn about budgeting?
• Could you explain how these two elephants differ?	• What do you think about these two elephants?

Figure 2.1 This chart compares specific questions with vague questions.

Wait Time

Critical – and creative – thinking skills and reflection take time to learn, although some students acquire these skills quickly. Unfortunately, it is often the same quick learners or the most talkative who are provided practice and exercise in these important skills. These students rapidly establish a pattern in the classroom: The teacher asks a thought-provoking question, and the "eager beavers" quickly and exuberantly have their hands up with an answer. The other students do not even have a chance to consider the question. Or, they delay raising their hands to avoid having to think about and answer the question. The quick-thinking few answer the majority of the questions, delighting the teacher with their ability to keep up a snappy pace, while the others sit by passively.

It is important that *every* learner be given time to consider the question. The teacher must invite the opinions and ideas of even the most reticent student and let it be known that everyone will have a chance to respond.

Rowe (reported in Bianchini 2008) explored wait time over a number of years in a multitude of studies across grade levels. She found that teachers, after asking a question, typically waited less than one second to call on a student. However, if teachers waited at least three seconds and as long as ten seconds, all children had enough time to think about an answer. A synthesis of Rowe's studies showed that students' responses became longer when the teacher waited at least three seconds for a response. More students volunteered (often changing teachers' judgments of "underachieving" students). Fewer students failed to respond at all. In addition, students' confidence in their answers increased, as did their ability to speculate. Students increased the rate of offering evidence and conclusions or inferences they had reached, and the number of student questions increased. Rowe also looked at wait time after a student answered the question and found it was critical in producing more student engagement.

Though three seconds may seem like a brief period of time, look at a watch or clock, and observe how long it is. Try waiting for 10 seconds. Because most of us are not accustomed to silence in a classroom, even three seconds can seem like an eternity. Sometimes, only a few students will have their hands up after three to ten seconds of wait time. When that happens, ask the question again, and make eye contact with some of the learners who do not have their hands up. (Do not reword a carefully crafted question, or students are apt to perceive it as a new question.) Pause for several seconds, then, if most learners have still not raised their hands, call on a student who has his or her hand up, and then another student, allowing more wait time for students who may still be thinking. You will get responses that other children can build upon. You should never have to answer your own questions.

Student Responses

Higher-order questions are usually complex and have more than one answer. Thus, more than one student may be called on to provide an answer, give an example, or elaborate on what another classmate has answered. A high-level question needs a high-level response or, rather, multiple high-level responses. A high-level response does the following:

- Answers all of the question
- Gives evidence, examples
- Is plausible
- Is original (not a repetition of what was in a book or what another student just said)

If a student has an incomplete answer or you are not sure what point he or she is making, you may need to probe or cue the student (Costa and Marzano 2001). For instance:

- Give me an example.
- Tell me a little more.
- Elaborate on what you have said.
- You answered the first part, what do you think about...?

Conducting "Grand Conversations"

To involve students in thinking, feeling, and responding to ideas, issues, events, and characters in a book, teachers must focus on questioning strategies that resemble "grand conversations" rather than the more common "gentle inquisitions" (Bird 1988; Edelsky 1988). Grand conversations enable students to express their ideas honestly and to share their thoughts and experiences with their classmates in meaningful ways. Grand conversations are most similar to the lively discussions that occur in adult book groups. In such groups, the focus is on the relevance and personal reactions of the participants, and every member is invited to take part.

During gentle inquisitions, on the other hand, the tone of the classroom interaction is usually one of checking with students to make sure they have read the book. The teacher dutifully asks the questions, the students dutifully answer them, the teacher then decides if the students have understood. While there is certainly a need for diagnosing student comprehension, studies show that an inordinate amount of time is spent in this kind of robotic assessment in lieu of richer literary discussions (Wendler, Samuels, and Moore 1989), and at the expense of time spent on critical thinking (Langer et al. 1990).

Student-Directed Discussions

One of the most detrimental behaviors to the critical and creative thinking of youngsters is when the teacher dominates the talk in a classroom. Uncomfortable with silence or with a pace perceived to be plodding, the teacher asks one question after another and adds extraneous information to the students' responses. This can confuse the students and allows them little time to think or connect ideas. By contrast, in a student-centered classroom, the teacher becomes "the guide on the side," rather than the "sage on the stage" – a true facilitator rather than the guru with all the answers. In such a classroom, a student may ask a question that another student will respond to. A third student may politely challenge the response or add additional perspective, while the teacher merely affirms and praises all the participants. For example:

> RENÉ: Why do camels have humps?
>
> TEACHER: Does anyone have any idea about that?
>
> RAUL: I think I read that they store food and water in their humps.
>
> GRACIELA: I think you are right, but some camels only have one hump. They must be the kind that have not far to go in the desert.
>
> RAUL: No, I think they're just a different breed, like cats that can have long furry tails, or Manxes that have no tails.
>
> TEACHER: You have raised some interesting questions. Why don't you look up camel on the Internet, and see what you can find out? Then get back to us.

Equality in the Classroom

When teachers ask questions, it is important they do not recognize students who randomly shout out responses. Instead, they should insist that students raise their hands and wait to be called upon before they respond. Though many teachers worry that such rules are unnecessarily rigid, and other teachers are delighted when they hear immediate responses shouted out, such behavior results in unequal interactions. Boys tend to be more vocal than girls in class, for example. Even at the college level, males are more vocal than their female counterparts, and, when allowed by the professor, dominate and interrupt their female peers. Additionally, children from certain cultural groups, such as the Vietnamese, are taught at home to be polite, quiet, and even self-effacing. They are usually overshadowed by children who choose to shout out answers (Davidman 1994). Therefore, every teacher should discourage students from shouting out answers, thereby ensuring more equal distribution of interaction time in the classroom.

A related issue is the tendency of teachers to call on the brighter students and give them more time to articulate their responses. A teacher who allows less time when calling on a slower student or who calls on students of one gender more than the other is showing a bias or a lack of confidence in certain students. This is detrimental in the effort to establish a positive, equal, and safe learning environment for all students. It is critical that teachers show confidence in all students and not discriminate among them.

Most teachers are committed to providing fair treatment to all their learners, and they are simply unaware of many seemingly discriminatory practices. To provide egalitarian instruction takes concentration and effort. But it is possible. Teachers can prepare a seating chart on a clipboard and make a mark next to a student's name as he or she is called upon. Also, teachers can practice giving equal wait time to all learners (place one hand behind your back, and slowly fold back your fingers one at a time, with each finger folded representing one second of wait time). Finally, an invited observer or a videotape of a lesson can allow a teacher the luxury of revisiting a lesson to focus on the fairness of the distribution of responses.

Appropriate Use of Praise

The use of strong praise is sometimes appropriate – when working with very young children, second-language learners who are just emerging from the "silent period" (the period during which they are first silent as they develop receptive language), children with special needs, or when asking questions of factual or low-level recall (for example, Jeff, what was the falcon's name?). But when the goal is to have the students think critically and creatively, the teacher should use strong praise for student responses with care, as it tends to squelch higher-level thinking (Bianchini 2008).

A strong praise response (active acceptance) is exemplified by a teacher who responds to a student's answer with, That's exactly right! Excellent job! Such praise encourages conformity. Students start to depend on the praise-giver for their worth, rather than on themselves and their own satisfaction with their ideas. Instead of praise, the goal should be to help students find intrinsic sources for their own motivation. When the teacher gives a passive acceptance response, such as, "Yes, that is one way to think about Kay's problem," he or she keeps the window open for further thinking on the part of others in the class.

Passive acceptance responses can also be used effectively in brainstorming sessions when, for example, the teacher says, After asking the question and giving you some time to think about it, I would like to hear everyone's ideas. I will write your ideas on the whiteboard (or SMART Board). Only after all the students' responses have been recorded does the class begin its consideration of each individual response. In the classroom, that kind of nonjudgmental acceptance of all ideas generates the greatest amount of critical and creative reflection.

Continually Encouraging Inquiry

We derive meaning and knowledge by asking questions. The ability to recognize problems and form questions is a skill – and the key to problem solving and the development of critical-thinking skills. It is the responsibility of teachers to encourage students to formulate questions and to help them word their questions so that possible answers can be sought, and found. This process is necessary to build a base of knowledge that can be called upon again and again as a way to connect, interpret, and assimilate new information in new situations.

Through constant practice in the use of questioning, students soon discover that inquiry is the cornerstone to critical thinking and real-world problem solving. They also realize that there are usually no absolute answers. Some answers are better than others, not correct or incorrect. Student must be taught to: (1) recognize the problem, (2) formulate a question about the problem (for example, Should I take ballet lessons or piano lessons? Should I sign up for soccer or get a paper route? Should I drink orange juice or a Coke?), (3) collect all the necessary data, and (4) arrive at a temporarily acceptable answer to the problem, while understanding that at some later time new data may call for modification of the conclusion.

Finally, by being told there is no such thing as a "dumb question," students are encouraged to ask questions about everything and anything. For instance, students (like everyone else) may ask questions that seem out of context with the content of a particular lesson or for which they could just as easily look up the answers themselves. Such questions consume precious class time, and, understandably, can frustrate the teacher. A teacher's initial reaction might be to quickly brush off the question, or to tell the student to look up the answer or to "stay on the subject." Such a reaction, however, can have a negative effect on the openness of the entire class. Instead of showing irritation, the teacher should answer kindly and professionally, and later try to zero in on the student's purpose for asking the question. At that time, the teacher can ask what the student thought about the question or how the question is related to the topic. Often a seemingly off-the-mark question has a connection to the discussion, but the student is not clear or sure of the connection. The question may signal a student's need for recognition and more interaction with the teacher. If this is the case, a possible response might be, You asked an interesting question, and I would like to discuss it with you. Could we meet together before or after school, or at recess, to talk?

Students' questions can and should be used as springboards for further questions, investigations, and discussions. Students should be encouraged to ask the entire spectrum of questions – questions that politely challenge the textbook, current practices, and others' statements (including the teacher's) – and to seek the facts or evidence behind a statement, practice, or policy. Jones and Leahy (2006) recommend that students keep "wonder notebooks." In wonder notebooks, students record new ideas and questions that occur to them throughout the day. For instance, while studying explorers, a student might wonder what would have happened if Columbus had landed on the west coast of North America. Teachers may also design a "wonder bulletin board." As students come up with ideas, the teacher can record the ideas on cards to display on the board. This may spark ideas from other students.

Admitting Lack of Knowledge

Nothing diminishes a teacher's credibility more than when students realize he or she has bluffed an answer to a question. Most children, especially very young ones, believe their teacher knows *everything* – more, even, than their parents. This is a tremendous burden for even the most well-informed teacher. No one, of course, knows everything. It is important, therefore, for teachers to admit when they do not know the answer to a question. This allows students to see that teachers, too, are human. It also gives students – regardless of their ability and without damaging their self-esteem – permission to not know all the answers. At the same time, it is important for teachers to demonstrate that they care about the question, know where and how to find possible answers to the question, and are willing to help students develop these same skills.

A CHECKLIST FOR CLASSROOM CLIMATE

Use the following questions as a checklist to determine if the atmosphere in your classroom is conducive to the free flow of questions and answers. Most of the questions relate to the activities presented in this book. The list is not exhaustive but, hopefully, will encourage you to generate other reflective questions to help you discover if you are creating a climate necessary for children to become deeply involved with questions.

- Am I providing an atmosphere that is non-threatening and that encourages all students to articulate the questions they really want to ask?
- Am I providing plenty of opportunities for students to discuss their ideas with their classmates and with me?
- Am I providing enough factual information first so that students have foundations for discussion?
- Am I offering specific suggestions to students about how to plan, organize, and implement particular question strategies for processing information?
- Do I schedule opportunities for students to react cognitively and affectively to questions encountered or planned?
- Do I plan questioning sessions so that my questions are clear and my vocabulary is appropriate to my learners?
- Do I avoid dominating the discussions?
- Do I call on several students to generate in-depth responses?
- Do I provide enough wait time so that all students have an opportunity to carefully consider the questions?
- Do I provide an equal opportunity for all learners to answer questions and participate in discussions?
- Do I, as the teacher, model good questioning?
- Am I open to new ways of organizing my classroom and doing things?
- Am I willing to admit that I do not have all the answers, and can I show children how to discover the answers to questions?

PART I
Summary

Asking good questions is essential when receiving information and ideas. In chapter 1, we explored the kinds of questions that are possible. We did this through the two taxonomies proposed by Benjamin Bloom. We then described each level of questioning and example questions for each level. The cognitive domain is considered the basic framework for all classroom questioning; the affective domain provides a complementary structure for many feelings, emotions, and values that are integral to learning. We also considered an expanded view of Bloom's Cognitive Taxonomy to help analyze and build skills for inquiry. The expanded model can help analyze what may be blocking students and employs strategies to help them succeed.

We also explored other types of questions that teachers ask for a variety of purposes. Teachers ask clarifying questions to understand what a child is really trying to say, cuing questions to give hints, focusing questions to direct the attention of learners, and probing questions to encourage children to elaborate beyond single-word responses. A caveat was issued regarding the practice of Initiate-Respond-Evaluate (IRE), which is prevalent in many elementary classrooms. While the level of critical discussion emanating from the use of IRE may be high, the danger comes when the teacher has already decided upon the answers to the questions. If a child's answer differs from the teacher's, or if the child is unable to match the teacher's cultural references, the child will not succeed in such a forum. Often teachers are not fully aware of their own IRE tactics. An excellent way to self-assess is to make videos of class discussions.

Some suggestions were also offered in chapter 1 on how the taxonomies of questions could be put to use in a variety of classroom situations. Finally, a short quiz gave you a way to determine if you are able to discriminate between the two domains of questioning and if you can recognize what level of mental processing would be at work if you were asked such questions.

Asking children the right questions so they will be fully involved in processing and applying knowledge and ideas may not be educational salvation, but it is certainly a step in the right direction. Yamamoto (1969, 61) once mused, "Each tree is known by its own fruit...and we cannot expect to gather figs from thorns or grapes from a bramble bush." Similarly, if we place a premium on only low-level, factual questions, we are then settling for the creation of passive learners. If, on the other hand, we involve children in answering critical and creative questions, and we prod them to carefully formulate their attitudes and beliefs, we contribute to their competence and support their search for their own human identity.

For children to feel safe and comfortable enough to enter into discussions where there is a free flow of questions and answers, the classroom climate must be conducive to lively interchange. In chapter 2, we explored a panoply of considerations for creating such a classroom.

The key factor in maintaining a positive atmosphere that fosters the free flow of questions and answers is *freedom*. It means that children are free to raise a wide range of questions, and free to pose questions that interest them. It means that the teacher accepts children's feelings, beliefs, and, occasionally, an off-the-mark question. It also means the teacher listens carefully to children and is enthusiastic in working with them so they process their questions. This free atmosphere may be structured in other ways, but it is always one in which the teacher and other children welcome and respect one another's ideas.

Finally, a free atmosphere for questioning is one in which the teacher and students demonstrate that they have confidence in each other. The teacher has enough confidence in the students to allow many discussions to be student-centered, and the students have enough confidence in the teacher that they participate fully in such discussions.

However, the teacher and students are both confident enough to admit they do not know *all* of the answers to *all* of the questions, but joyfully share in the knowledge gained in their discoveries. In such a classroom, there is no such thing as a dumb question. In fact, the level of questions asked rises dramatically as the exemplar of good questioning in this classroom – the teacher – continually stimulates the critical and creative thinking of each and every child.

PART II
Questioning Strategies

The question is a pivotal – if not *the* pivotal – component in promoting higher-order thinking and critical thinking. Whether you are functioning at a thinking level or at a feeling level with data, you need to generate well-constructed questions. As a teacher, the questions you create and the manner in which you phrase and sequence them strongly influence the quality, significance, and accuracy of the learners' conclusions and how students use those conclusions.

Becoming adept at asking questions is an important but deceptively difficult skill to learn. Uncovering the many dimensions of inquiry, the numerous questioning strategies, and your role in them take time and practice. But it is time well spent, for it provides students with access to experiences with critical thinking that they can use for the rest of their lives.

Since the question is the linchpin to meaningful engagement with learning, teachers need to be good questioners and be able to provide students with formal and informal situations in which they can learn about the realm of questions and questioning.

* * *

One rich source for questions is often overlooked – the students. Barell (2003) and Noddings (2008) assert that all discussions be student-centered, giving *all* children the opportunity to freely express their thoughts and opinions. In reality, teachers do most of the talking and questioning. This is unfortunate. Costa (2001) and Swartz (2008) find students attain significantly higher levels of thinking when they are encouraged to develop skill in generating critical and creative questions and when they are provided opportunities for dialogue with classmates about the questions posed and conclusions derived from information they encounter.

Cornbleth (1975) presents some compelling evidence to support student questioning:

- All students can be encouraged to ask productive or critical questions.
- The more questions a student asks in any one time period, the greater the probability that the questions will be higher level.
- Students become more actively engaged in classes where they are encouraged to ask their own questions.

Nor should student self-questioning be overlooked as a viable strategy (Van Hof 2009). Self-questioning strategies teach children to ask their own questions as they read. Mason and Au (1986, 157) explore the value of self-questioning:

> To be able to ask questions, students must be actively thinking about and working with the text. In asking their own pre-questions, that is, questions about material not yet read, students decide what the selections might be about and what they might want to learn from it. This gives students a chance to set their own purposes for reading.

Jackson (2001) concludes that self-discovery questions help students strengthen their sense of identity and affect their motivation to achieve. Clearly, self-questioning can enhance comprehension both by encouraging active involvement and by giving children authentic experiences in setting their own purposes for reading and examining life experiences. Finally, teaching children to construct their own questions can greatly improve retention of both narrative and expository material (Singer and Donlon 1982; Balajthy 1983).

In the following chapters, we present a series of teacher-tested questioning strategies. In chapters 3 and 4, we respond to the query, How can I model good questioning strategies that will help my students think more critically? It is important to understand the basic reason for each strategy and to have a general idea of how that strategy is used in the context of a lesson in a real classroom. To this end, we provide a selection of exemplary strategies that you can use to model effective questions. These have been designed to show children how to develop conceptual frameworks for thinking critically in both the affective and cognitive domains.

In chapters 5 and 6, we explore several strategies that you can use to promote self-questioning strategies in your students. The goals of each strategy are to help children think more critically and creatively while reading and reflecting on experiences, and to help students become more proficient at setting appropriate purposes and expectations for reading and experiences. Any of these strategies can be used as a refreshing alternative to more traditional, teacher-dominated reading and learning activities.

The main focus of these chapters is on student independence. The real power of these questioning strategies will come when children are competent in using them, on their own, as necessary. Therefore, as you teach these critical strategies, it is important to show children how much they will increase their ability to understand what they read and experience. Children are *most* likely to internalize these strategies when they have had repeated opportunities to use them successfully in a variety of learning situations. Your students are then on their way to becoming highly proficient critical thinkers and readers.

All the strategies are presented in a consistent form: a rationale, a general description, and an example of the strategy used within the context of an actual lesson. In many instances, related information or an activity sheet is provided.

* * *

The ability to construct meaning from text and to gain content knowledge is enhanced both by thinking about and by engaging in cross-curricular learning. In most content areas (Beyer 2001; Roberts and Billings 2008; Swartz 2008), the process of constructing meaning has many of the same characteristics. Children construct meaning when the following happen:

- What they are studying is authentic and important to them
- What they are learning integrates all the language arts – reading, writing, listening, speaking – as well as thinking
- Their prior knowledge is tapped
- Interrelationships between new knowledge and old knowledge, one curricular area and the other, are pointed out to them
- They have the support in *any* curricular area. Effective questions provide a way for teachers to offer this valuable assistance.

In chapter 7, we explore how questioning strategies can be used across the entire elementary curriculum, exhorting children to think critically and creatively in all content areas.

SOME GUIDELINES FOR USING QUESTIONING STRATEGIES

Before using questioning strategies in the classroom, teachers will find the following guidelines helpful:

- Use strategies on the basis of your students' needs. Though the strategies are all motivational and teacher-tested, do not use them indiscriminately. Some students will have already picked up many effective reading and thinking strategies through their own experiences; they will not need the benefit of specific coaching in asking and answering questions. Use the questioning strategies only when you observe that meaning construction would be enhanced by a lesson on specific questioning techniques.
- Introduce each questioning strategy in the context of an authentic educational experience. Historically, there has been an unfortunate tendency for teachers to use strategies as isolated skills, dooming them to a reception of apathy and, eventually, failure. An authentic educational experience occurs when you (1) select motivational experiences and reading material from the integrated curriculum with which to use the strategy, (2) use these materials as the vehicle through which to model the strategy, and (3) find other appropriate reading materials and experiences with which the students may practice the strategy.

- Introduce only one questioning strategy at a time. To teach questioning strategies thoroughly, it is important that they be continually reinforced through practice with a variety of authentic reading and learning experiences. The application of any new strategy is often difficult for children until it has been comfortably internalized; a lot of practice with one strategy at a time is the key to success.

- Use scaffolding to introduce the strategies. Be explicit with steps of a strategy. As you use the strategy in other situations, reduce the clues and cues. Ask students to recall what they did in similar circumstances.

- Ensure that each student is successful using the strategy. "Nothing succeeds like success." Children will feel successful using the questioning strategies if they have many opportunities to share how the strategies worked for them and if you point out their successes.

- Relate strategies and information to students' lives. Have students generate their own examples (Costa 2001). Ask students to apply knowledge and skills to new situations.

- Strive to transfer the responsibility of the questioning strategies from you to the students. In most of the questioning strategies, you must first model how the strategy is applied to reading materials and experiences. Once the students feel comfortable using a strategy, you should fade from the picture and let students model it for each other, eventually using it independently. If, however, it becomes clear that more modeling is needed, reintroduce the strategy and provide guided practice, but return the responsibility to the students as quickly as possible (Cooper 1993).

CHAPTER 3
Teacher Questioning Strategies for Primary Grades

Many educators still seem to believe that both critical thinking and asking and answering higher-order questions are skills reserved for children in grade four and beyond. Nothing could be further from the truth! The reality is that the sooner students realize that there are many ways of thinking about an issue, the more likely it is that they will grow up with the freedom to look at the world in a variety of ways.

The strategies offered in this chapter can be taught to children as young as kindergarten-age, if no actual written response is required. Strategies that ask for written responses can be used as soon as students have the written proficiency to answer the questions, or the questions may be asked and answered orally. Though suggested for the primary grades, these strategies are also appropriate for older students, particularly those who have had little previous practice in thinking critically.

KNOWLEDGE CHART

Rationale

Teachers use guided questions to show students how to access their background knowledge, or schema. They then help students identify their new knowledge in a given subject by placing it on a chart. Modeled after a procedure developed by Ogle (1986), Knowledge Chart strategy can be used both before and after reading or listening to a selection that contains factual information. Students are more likely to remember and recall information from a text when they use this activity, because it activates their schema, or framework of expectations, for the subject and provides a slot in which to assimilate new ideas. Moreover, the students' involvement and enthusiasm appear to increase when this technique is used (Yopp and Yopp 1992).

Description

Draw five columns on the whiteboard, and title the columns as follows: *Knowledge, Questions, New Knowledge, Research*, and *Reactions*. (Students in middle years and up can fill in their own activity sheets. See figure 3.1.) Pick a topic, then have students generate a list of all they know about that topic. Invite the students to ask questions about the topic; these questions serve as the guiding purposes for reading or listening. Next, read information about the chosen topic to the students, then record in the third column what they have learned about the subject as a result of having read or listened to the book or passage. (Students who are interested in the topic can use questions that have not been answered as questions for further research.) The fifth column is sometimes used to record reactions to learning that are particularly interesting, unusual, or unexpected. The procedure, in outline form, goes like this:

1. Knowledge. Ask students, What do you know about [the topic]? Record all responses in the first column.

2. Questions. Ask, What would you like to know about [the topic]? Record the students' responses in the second column.

3. New Knowledge. After the reading about the topic, ask, What have you learned about [the topic]? Have students revise knowledge listed in the first column, answer questions from the second column, and, in the third column, list new information that had not been considered prior to the reading.

4. Research. Distribute student-initiated questions from the second column that have not been answered to students who are interested in doing additional research. Record their responses in the fourth column.

5. Reactions. Ask a question that will lead students to a personal evaluation, such as, How did this story change your feelings or thinking about [the topic]? Record students' responses in the fifth column.

Example

Before they read about kookaburras, the teacher asked her second-grade students, What do you know about kookaburras? She wrote the students' responses in the first column of the knowledge chart:

- It's an animal.
- They are found in zoos.
- They live in gum trees.
- There is a song about them.

Next, the teacher asked, Is there anything you would like to know about kookaburras? She wrote the students' responses in the second column of the knowledge chart:

- What do they eat?
- Where do they live?
- Do they make good pets?

THE KNOWLEDGE CHART

Name: _Sarah, Charles, José_   Date: _Oct. 25_

Topic: _Seahorses_

Knowledge	Questions	New Knowledge	Research	Reactions
What do you know about _Seahorses_?	What do you want to know about _Seahorses_?	What did you discover after reading about _Seahorses_?	What do you still want to know about _Seahorses_?	How do you now think or feel about _Seahorses_?
The seahorse is not really a horse. They live in salty seas. They're fish. They have curly tails. They hang onto weeds. They are very tiny. They don't swim in schools.	Where can you find them? What do they eat? Are they endangered? Could you keep them as pets? What are their predators? Do they come in different colors?	Male seahorses give birth and care for the young. Both eyes can see independently. They live in coral reefs, sea grass beds, and mangroves. There are 35 different kinds, or species. They are endangered. They are used for food, medicine, and decoration in many countries. Pollution is destroying the seahorse's habitat. Their predators are larger fish, crabs, and water birds.	Do they have live babies? How can we keep them from becoming extinct? How can we clean up their habitat? If the males give birth, are they really males? How long do they live?	I am more curious about them. I feel sad that they are losing their habitat. We are going to write a letter to the president to ask him to stop polluting coastal waters where the seahorses live.

Figure 3.1 This Knowledge Chart activity sheet was filled in by grade-five students who were learning about seahorses.

See BLM 1 in appendix for reproducible master.

- Are they friendly?
- What kind of animal are they?
- Do they have fur?
- Who are their enemies?
- Can you keep them as pets?

Then, the teacher reviewed the questions that the students had asked and had them read the following paragraph to see if they could find the answers to their questions:

> The kookaburra lives in Australia. It lives in the forest in small groups. Kookaburras are very friendly. They will accept food from people. Sometimes they even tap on windows hoping that people will feed them. Kookaburras eat insects, crabs, fish, and small birds. They are also quite famous as snake killers.

After the reading, the teacher asked the students to revisit the knowledge chart to see if any of their original understandings about kookaburras had changed (no). She then asked them if any of their questions about kookaburras had been answered (three had, and students could make inferences about others from the information in the passage).

At this point, the teacher asked the students to share some entirely new information they had learned about kookaburras from reading the passage. She listed their responses in the third column of the knowledge chart:

- They are famous snake killers.
- They beg for food.
- They live in small groups.

Of the original questions that the students had asked, at least two were not answered at all. A group of interested students either checked the Internet or went to the library to search for the answers to the following questions noted in the knowledge chart:

- What kind of animal are they?
- Do they have fur?
- Who are their enemies?
- Can you keep them as pets?

Finally, to learn about the students' reactions to the passage, the teacher asked, How did reading this paragraph change your thinking or feelings about the kookaburra? In the fifth column of the chart, she wrote the students' responses:

- I heard the kookaburra song before, and I had always wondered what that was.
- Now I know it's a funny animal.
- I want to read more about kookaburras!
- I think from reading that Australia must be a cool place.

- I want to go there sometime.
- I want to go to the zoo and see if they have a real kookaburra.
- I used to think kookaburra was just a weird word; now, I can imagine what one looks like.

Related Information

It is important for teachers to restrict the use of the Knowledge Chart strategy to books that contain factual information, or those with expository text. For example, children gain little, if any, accurate information about bears from reading *Goldilocks and the Three Bears*, which is narrative text. However, some works of fiction, or narrative text, do contain factual information in a most palatable format. In *The Secret Garden*, for instance, children learn much about the English moors. Thus, teachers must be familiar with the reading material and certain that it provides accurate factual information about the topic before using it as a subject for a knowledge chart.

RESPONSE HEURISTIC

Rationale

When teachers have students write in reading response or dialogue journals, they are often frustrated at their students' lack of personal involvement in the story or passage. Students often parrot, rather than react to, the events in a story. For example, a student might write, "Leslie hit her head on a rock while crossing the river" instead of "Leslie died, and I felt I had lost a friend. It reminded me of how sad and lonely I felt when my grandmother died." By modeling the appropriate critical questions that students should be asking, teachers can encourage their students to respond to the text on a deeper and more personal level. The Response Heuristic, developed by Bleich (1978), provides a means for students to analyze their own thoughts and feelings and helps them get into the habit of asking pertinent questions as they read.

Description

This questioning strategy involves three components: perceptions, reactions, and associations. It is helpful to introduce the strategy by modeling it with a story that has just been read to or by students. Students then give personal responses to each questioning component: (1) perceptions (What is important in the book?), (2) reactions (How does the story make you feel?), and (3) associations (What experiences have you had that the story reminds you of?).

After an initial teacher-modeled, shared reading experience using this technique, your students can write their own responses, using an activity sheet (see figure 3.2). Encourage students to share their responses, and affirm it is possible to have many different "correct" responses to the same material.

Example

A third-grade class listened as the teacher read *The Quiltmaker's Gift* by Jeff Brumbeau, a story about a king who is rich but not happy. The following is one student's reaction to the story:

Perceptions

TEACHER: What is important in the book?

STUDENT: The king had many, many riches, but he did not have all of the beautiful things in his kingdom – he did not have a quilt from the quiltmaker. She would only give her quilts to poor people, so the king could not get one.

Reactions

TEACHER: How did the story make you feel?

STUDENT: I was happy at the end of the story, but in the middle of the story I was very worried about the quiltmaker. I was surprised that the king really changed when he gave his things away. I remembered how I felt when I gave some of my toys and books to my younger cousin. At first I did not want to, but then I saw how happy he was, and I felt happy, too.

RESPONSE HEURISTIC

Name: _____Claudia_____   Date: ____December 10____

Theme: ____Ramona Quimby, Age 8, by Beverly Cleary____

1. What is important in the book?

Ramona has to do lots of things she has never done before. She's trying to be brave but it's hard for her.

2. How does the story make you feel?

I feel sorry for Ramona when she was getting so upset. She had to put up with her four year old sister too. I felt proud of Ramona that she could do it when the old man said she had a nice family, I was happy for Ramona.

3. What experiences have you had that the story reminds you of?

When my mother had to go back to work we all had to stick together. I didn't like it when she was never home when I got there. I can understand how Ramona felt.

See BLM 2 in appendix for reproducible master.

Figure 3.2 Students in intermediate grades can fill in their own Response Heuristic activity sheets.

Associations

TEACHER: What experiences have you had that the story reminds you of?

STUDENT: After I gave my cousin some of my things, my mom thought we still had too many toys. She said that for every new toy we got, we had to give one away. We could decide who would receive our toys. My brother and I decided to give our toys to a homeless shelter. When I think about the children there I am a little sad, but I hope my toys have made them smile.

CONCEPT FORMATION

Rationale

Concepts provide the building blocks of different discipline areas. Concept Formation gives students a powerful tool for understanding and applying information (Sternberg 2003). Concepts are formed when two or more objects, events, or ideas are grouped together on the basis of at least one similar characteristic. Having students gather items together based on like attributes – categorizing – helps them learn to recognize important characteristics. Concept Formation is a first step toward concept attainment – the ability to identify salient characteristics and distinguish examples from non-examples.

Description

To introduce Concept Formation in the classroom, give students a number of different items, ask them to identify attributes of those items, then have them group the items together based on one or more of the like attributes. The strategy follows the three steps described below.

1. List. Show students a group of items, and have them identify each.
2. Group. Have students select attributes by which the items can be categorized. Your students may group and re-group the same items based on different attributes. By grouping and re-grouping, students' observation skills are stretched. This enables them to take note of more and more details.
3. Label. Ask students to give each attribute, or category, a name.

Example

In this class, students were given several words that they were expected to study, remember, and recite on a test. Instead of having the students learn the words by writing them out, using the Cloze method, and/or completing word searches and crossword puzzles, the teacher introduced Concept Formation.

To begin, the teacher handed out cards to small groups of 3-4 students. Each group was given the same set of words, with one word on each card. Groups spread out the cards and read all of the words: fancy, any, lovely, story, party, penny, carry, monkey, city, very, angry, goofy, ugly, slippery, toasty, tea, bee.

TEACHER: Look at all of the words. In your groups, pick attributes or characteristics that you can use to categorize the words. Put all of the words that have a particular attribute into the same group. For example, I might put *carry* and *city* together, because they both start with the letter *c*.

JENNY: In our group, we have separated our words into two categories. In the first category, we have the words *any, angry, bee, carry, city, goofy, lovely,* and *monkey.* In the second category, we put the words *story, party, penny, very, ugly, slippery, toasty,* and *tea.*

JABAR: In our group, we have separated the words into five categories. In category one, we put *fancy, any, party, carry,* and *angry.* Two has the words *lovely, story, monkey, goofy,* and *toasty.* Three has *penny, very, bee,* and *tea.* Four has *city* and *slippery,* and *ugly* is in category five.

TEACHER: Now, give each of your word groups a name. The name for my example is words beginning with the letter *c*.

JENNY: Our categories are words that begin with letters in the first half of the alphabet and words that begin with letters in the last half of the alphabet.

JABAR: We grouped our words by looking at the first vowel in the word. We have put all the words with *a* together, then *o, e, i,* and *u.*

TEACHER: Let's see if you can come up with other ways of categorizing your words. Push all of the cards back together, and make new groups.

GLORIA: We put words together by the number of syllables: one syllable – *bee* and *tea;* two syllables – *fancy, any, lovely, story, party, penny, carry, monkey, city, very, angry, goofy,* and *ugly;* and three syllables – *slippery.*

JOSÉ: We regrouped the way we use the words in sentences. Naming words are *story, party, penny, monkey, tea, bee,* and *city. Carry* is an action word, and describing words are *fancy, any, lovely, very, angry, goofy, ugly,* and *slippery.*

TEACHER: How did you look at spelling words differently today?

TIKI: I noticed more details and patterns in the words. This was a fun way to look at spelling words.

MONIQUE: I even thought of even more categories. I like these words.

TEACHER: Can you think of some other times when you might use this strategy to learn words?

ELI: When we are learning new words in social studies, we can see if those words are like the words we are learning at spelling time.

MARY: If we are reading a new book or story, we can write down words that are new to us, and see if they are like some of our spelling words.

POLAR OPPOSITES

Rationale

This questioning activity is ideal for helping students see characters in texts as three-dimensional. This is done by asking them to assess characters on a variety of traits, using a three-, five-, or seven-point scale, depending on the grade level of the students. (It is difficult enough for young children to pick one of three choices; older children can judge more nuances of meaning on a five- or seven-point scale.) The exercise is most conducive to critical thinking when students are also asked to justify their responses. In other words, if they rate a character "generous" rather than "frugal," the teacher asks them why they believe this to be so, reminding them to cite evidence from the selection read to support their position.

Description

To initiate Polar Opposites, choose a character from a story that all the students are familiar with, and develop a list of personality traits that describes that character. Then, determine an opposite quality for each trait. For example, if a character is quiet and thoughtful and likes to be alone, you might write on one side of the chart *loner, quiet,* and *considerate.* On the opposite side of the chart, you might include the words *fun-loving, noisy,* and *inconsiderate.* Each pair of opposites comprises its own continuum, with three, five, or seven spaces in between (see figure 3.3). The students (as a group or individually) must determine where on the continuum each character falls. You then read the story or passage, and ask the students the following for each character, Where do you think [character] fits on this character chart? Why do you think so? What in the story supports your answer?

Example

A grade-three teacher read *Miss Maggie,* by Cynthia Rylant, to her students. The book is about Nat, a young boy who has heard stories about the reclusive elderly lady who lives in the log hut on his family's property. A big black snake, among other scary things, is reputed to live with her. Nat, initially fearing Miss Maggie, looks in her window and then runs away. One day, he overcomes his fears when he finds her in trouble. It is the middle of winter, and she is without heat. He finds her sitting on the floor of her cabin clutching a dead starling. He runs to get help for her. His family begins taking care of her and taking her with them on outings. Nat establishes a special, caring relationship with Miss Maggie.

After the reading, the activity sheet (see figure 3.3) was completed by some of the students.

POLAR OPPOSITES CHART

Name: _Hoa, Jared, Michael, Emily_   Date: _March 22_

Theme: _Miss Maggie_

Where do you think _____ **Nat** _____ would fit on this chart for each of the traits? Why?

1. brave ___ ___ ___ **X** ___ fearful

   We think Nat was fearful at first but he overcame his fear when he went to Miss Maggie's house.

2. cautious ___ ___ **X** ___ adventurous

   Nat was very cautious. Even though he went in Miss Maggie's house, it said his heart was pounding in his chest. We don't think he likes exploring.

3. wise ___ ___ ___ ___ **X** foolish

   Nat was foolish to believe all these things about Miss Maggie that were all lies. But he was wise enough to change his mind and care about her later.

4. happy ___ ___ ___ **X** ___ sad

   You don't ever see Nat laughing or having fun but he doesn't seem unhappy anywhere.

5. generous ___ ___ **X** ___ ___ greedy

   Nat is very generous to share his family and their love with Miss Maggie.

6. leader ___ ___ ___ ___ **X** follower

   Nat shouldn't listen to what people say so much or he could have had Miss Maggie as a wonderful friend much sooner.

Figure 3.3 This Polar Opposites activity sheet was completed by a small group of students after they had read the book *Miss Maggie*. The teacher created a five-point scale for students to choose from.

POINT OF VIEW AND OBSERVATION

Rationale

An important skill in narrative reading is the ability to determine the point of view of a story. Historians strive for objectivity, leaving out personal points of view. Scientists often have a research focus; for instance, educators may study and write from a behavioral, a cognitive or developmental, or a humanistic perspective. When studying art, students need to take into account perspective in creating and appreciating art. Younger children need concrete experiences that help them develop a foundation for understanding point of view.

Description

The procedure for this strategy is as follows:

1. Explain to students that proximity, distance, and values may affect or change what they see. You are going to show them a strategy they can use to help them understand points of view.

2. Select an item (or event) that you want students to observe. You may want to begin outside on the playground (when recess is not in session) to eliminate too many distractions.

3. Place the selected item where it is not easily observed from all locations (for example, behind a sandbox, next to a bike rack). Make sure students have not seen where the item has been placed.

4. When all students are together, point out where the item has been placed.

5. Have students describe what they see from varying distances (for example, 100 feet [30 meters] away, 50 feet [15 meters], 10 feet [3 meters], 2 feet [61 centimeters]).

6. As a class, discuss how distance changes the way one sees something.

Repeat the exercise (1) using different items and (2) observing from different perspectives (for example, moving in a circle around an item).

Example

In this classroom, the teacher contrived a situation that initiated the following discussion:

TEACHER: Today our pet hamster got out of its cage. Who was sitting near the cage and observed what happened?

JAMIE: The cage door was open. The hamster crawled out the door and down the cupboard.

JOHN: It felt funny on my foot.

TEACHER: Did you observe "funny"?

JOHN: Oh, he ran over my foot.

TEACHER: Jamie and John were sitting close to the hamster. Did anyone else see anything?

MARIA: I couldn't see anything, but I heard talking and saw people moving around, but I didn't know what was happening.

TEACHER: I want you all to draw a picture of your observations – what you saw or what you heard. I'll give you several minutes to draw your pictures, then have you hold up your illustration for all to see.

TEACHER (*After each student has held up his or her picture.*): What do you notice about the pictures?

EMILE: The pictures drawn by those closest to the cage, like John and Jamie, have lots of details.

MANNY: The people who are farther away from the cage do not have very many details in their pictures.

TEACHER: Why do you think the pictures are so different?

EMILE: People who were closer to the cage were able to see what happened.

TEACHER: That's true. Another reason why pictures are so different could be that some of you like animals more than others and want to include more information in your picture. So, sometimes we have more information about an item or event because we are closer to what happened, or we have a better view of what happened than someone else. Sometimes, if we like something or do not like it, we may see it differently....So far, we have used pictures to show what we have seen. How can we describe what we have seen using words? We need to use different words when we are sure of something we have seen and when we are not so sure. Can you give me some examples of words we can use when we're not so sure?

JORGE: When we're not sure, we could say things like, I think I saw..., Perhaps..., or It may have been....

TEACHER: Can you give me some examples of words we can use when we are sure?

RITA: We could say something like, I saw five.... or I heard this... or I counted ten....

MULTIPLE RESPONSE

Rationale

The Multiple Response strategy (Orlich et al. 2009) is a logical precursor to student-conducted discussions. Student discussions, however, are difficult to use effectively, because young children do not always possess the needed discussion behaviors or skills. By using multiple response questions, the teacher subtly conditions the students to accept more and more responsibility for listening to one another and for modifying modeled responses. Additionally, by using divergent or critical questions coupled with the Multiple Response strategy, the teacher has a unique opportunity to (1) analyze the types of responses that are being given, and (2) make a qualitative evaluation of each learner's response.

Description

When using the Multiple Response strategy, at least three or four students answer a given question. The key to increasing the number of students who respond to a question is to ask a divergent (creative) or evaluative (critical) question, or a question that is open-ended. By doing this, you can predict there will be more than one response or that responses will not duplicate one another. Moreover, you will not have a preconceived notion of what the *correct* answer should be. Proceed with the strategy as follows:

1. Create either a divergent or evaluative question.

2. Pose the question to the students.

3. Provide adequate time (at least three seconds) for all learners to consider the question, articulate a response, and raise their hands.

4. Identify three or four students to offer responses. Write students' responses on the whiteboard to provide them with visual cues and affirmation. Provide a three-second wait-time after students respond to the question.

5. Remind students to listen carefully to their classmates' responses so they will not repeat what has been previously offered. However, students may add to what another student answers by providing more details, elaborating on an example, providing some backup, or giving another example.

6. After the students have responded, provide them with affirmations (for example, to one student for providing the most complete response, to another for the most original response, and to another for giving reasons and examples in the response).

Example

A second-grade teacher used the Multiple Response strategy to encourage students to listen to one another as they considered a critical-thinking question.

TEACHER: Today, I'm going to try something new. I'll ask a question and wait for a minute for everyone to think about it, and then I'll call on four of you to respond. You will need to listen very carefully, because I will not repeat the question. Also, you will need to listen very carefully to your classmates as they answer so that you don't repeat what they have said. (*Asks a student to paraphrase the instructions to be sure everyone understands.*) Here goes. (*Asks question in anticipation for a unit on eyesight.*) Why do you think we have two eyes instead of only one? (*Pauses.*) José, Gina, Chrissy, and Hoa.

JOSÉ: Well, we have two arms and two legs and even two eyebrows. I think we would look silly with just one eye! (*Teacher nods head, smiles, and points to Gina without commenting.*)

GINA: Yeah, but we only have one nose and one mouth. We're used to it being that way. What if we had two mouths? (*The other students laugh. The teacher nods and points to Chrissy.*)

CHRISSY: Because God made us this way. That's the only reason why.

HOA: Well, maybe God made us with two eyes in case one didn't work. My uncle is blind in one eye. If he didn't have another eye he would not be able to see at all.

TEACHER: Those are all interesting ideas. Let's go to the library and see what we can find out about our eyesight. I will check the encyclopedia. Graciela, you can look on the Internet. Jacques, try to find a trade book about our eyes and eyesight.

RECIPROCAL TEACHING

Rationale

Reciprocal Teaching, developed by Palinscar and Brown (1984), encourages students to monitor their own comprehension while reading expository text. It also encourages students to be active in the process of constructing meaning from texts. Proficient readers often stop during the reading of expository text to determine what questions have been answered and what new questions have arisen as a result of the reading, even though such questions are asked instantaneously and subconsciously. Through Reciprocal Teaching, students can be shown that while questions can be answered by reading, reading often generates new questions. Sporer, Brunstein, and Kieschke (2009) used Reciprocal Teaching in pairs and small groups and compared student achievement to traditional reading methods. Students were engaged in specific skills of predicting, questioning, clarifying, and summarizing (Jones and Leahy 2006). Students in the Reciprocal Teaching groups had significant gains in standardized reading achievement tests. Pilonieta and Medina (2009) specifically adapted Reciprocal Teaching to primary grades in a 24-week program described below.

Description

During Reciprocal Teaching, model the comprehension activity, and then have the students attempt the same activity. Give students feedback on their performances. Specifically, the outline of the procedure is as follows:

Part 1: Introduce Individual Strategies

Pre-Reading:

1. Picture walk: Show pictures to students.
2. Make predictions about content.
3. Set the purpose. (What are we trying to find out?)

During Reading:

1. With the students, read a passage of expository text aloud.
2. Ask the group an important question about the text – one that focuses on the key issue (what, where, why, who, when, how).
3. Model this question-asking process for the students many times.

Post Reading:

1. Clarify content.
2. Visualize the most important part of the text.

Part 2: Fishbowl

Choose seven students who are reading leaders. Give one cue card to each student (the cues, based on the actions below, are: picture walk, predictions, purpose, clarifying, generating questions, visualizing, and summarizing). Have the remaining students observe as you guide the seven students through the following steps:

1. Picture-walk leader tells students to take a picture walk.
2. Predictions leader asks group for prediction suggestions, uses group feedback to make own predictions, shares with whole group.
3. Purpose leader asks group for suggestions of purpose, uses those suggestions to formulate purpose, and shares with whole group.
4. Buddy read and whole-class choral read.
5. Clarifier gives two words that are hard to read or understand.
6. Questioner asks the group for questions, formulates two questions from those suggestions, and asks the group the questions.
7. Visualizer shares a picture of the most important part of the selection.
8. Summarizer tells a shorter version of the selection.

Model, affirm correct responses, ask probing questions, and, generally, offer feedback to the seven students.

Part 3: Group to Teacher

Students can ask the teacher questions (reciprocate).

Name each student who participated in the fishbowl as the leader of a small group. Have each group follow the process described in Part 2. At the same time, circulate, and cue the leaders and groups as needed. Have students keep the same roles for several rotations to ensure practice and accomplishment.

Part 4: Independent Groups

Have students practice Reciprocal Teaching by playing different roles.

Part 5: Writing – Individual Accountability

Pilonieta and Medina (2009) describe this step as optional.

In all of these activities, together with your students, select from four main critical-thinking strategies: (1) summarize the section that was read, (2) predict what the next section will be about, (3) ask a question about the main idea of the section that was read, and (4) ask a question that helps to clarify the meaning of the passage.

Example

The following dialogue between a teacher and a small group of third-grade students who had read the first section of a passage about koala bears indicates the type of progress that can be made using Reciprocal Teaching.

JARED: What is found in Australia and also eats eucalyptus leaves and they have...? No, this isn't right.

TEACHER: Do you want to ask a question about koala bears?

JARED: Yeah.

TEACHER: Well, what would be a good question to ask about them that starts with the word *why*?

JARED: Why do they want to be koala bears? No....

TEACHER: You're on the right track. Try again.

JARED: Why are they called *koala bears*?

TEACHER: There you go. They are called koala bears because, even though they aren't bears, they look like little bears. Would they make good pets?

MARTA: No, even though they are cute, they are wild animals, and they live in trees. My turn? Are they extinct? Are they in danger of becoming extinct?

TEACHER: Marta has some interesting questions. Marta, you will be in the fishbowl group for the rest of the story. Will you be the "questioner" for the next section and ask two questions? Matt, would you take us on a picture walk? Clara, would you make some predictions? Ben, would you find two words that are new or need clarification? At the end of the passage, Lita, would you visualize the most important parts of the story, and, Sammy, would you summarize and give us the highlights of the passage? I want everyone to watch what this group does, because you will all be in a small group for the next section and have one of these roles.

MATT [picture walk]: The pictures seem to be about the environment of the koalas.

CLARA [predictions]: I think we will learn about their natural environment and what they have to have in zoos.

JUAN [purpose]: I asked my group members about the purpose of the story. I thought about their suggestions and came up with this purpose: It is to learn about animals that we do not see often.

BEN [clarify]: I think the two clarifying words are *herbivores* and *marsupial*.

MARTA [questions]: My questions are: Are they extinct? Are they in danger of becoming extinct?

LITA [visualize]: I think the most important part of the story is that a koala bear eats 400 to 500 grams of eucalyptus leaves a day. I found a jar that shows this amount.

SAMMY [summary]: To understand any animal, we have to know what its basic needs are and if its environment makes those needs easily available.

GROUP (*To teacher.*): Do you have any questions to ask us? About the roles? About what we have read so far?

TEACHER: How is the purpose role different from the summarizer? I would also like to know what each of you thinks now. Everyone can write a paragraph that summarizes the selection we just read. You may use ideas that the group discussed. (*After all students have written a paragraph.*) Now, everyone in the class gets to use these roles to look at the next section. I am going to assign each of you to a group and a role. Everyone who was in the fishbowl group will be in a new group. In your groups, read the next section. When everyone is ready, we will meet together as a class and discuss the passage. We will be using this method to study other science topics.

PROBABLE PASSAGES

Rationale

Wood's article "Probable Passages: A Writing Strategy" (1987) is a teacher-modeled prediction strategy that integrates writing and critical thinking with the reading of narrative selections. Such a strategy enables students to use their understanding of the six story elements – setting, beginning, problem, attempt, outcome, and original story ending – to construct text using key words provided by the teacher. This strategy features a unique marriage of story grammar knowledge and pre-reading prediction to encourage critical thinking.

Description

Probable Passages is divided into four stages: (1) preparation stage, (2) pre-reading stage, (3) reading stage, and (4) post-reading stage. The strategy is conducted in the following manner:

1. Preparation stage. On a whiteboard, write *Key Words, Story Frame,* and *Blank Probable Passage*. Select a passage of narrative (story) text, and pick out words that are important to the problem. List these words under Key Words. Next, write the six story elements under Story Frame. Under Blank Probable Passage, set up a fill-in-the-blanks passage. This passage must include the six story elements:

   The story takes place [setting]. [Beginning] is a character in the story who
   _____. A problem occurs when [problem]. Then [attempt]. The
   problem is solved when [outcome]. The story ends [ending].

2. Pre-reading stage. Read the key words aloud, and ask the students to repeat them. Ask these questions, What do you think a story that uses these words is going to be about? How would these words fit into the story frame? Help the students use the words from the story frame to complete a logical probable passage.

3. Reading stage. Have the students read the selection to find out how close their predictions match the actual story.

4. Post-reading stage. Ask, "How did your 'probable passage' compare with the plot of the story?" Have students revise their probable passages to reflect the actual story plot. (Note: Often the students' probable passages turn out to be more interesting stories than the actual one. Point this out.)

Example

A second-grade class used the Probable Passages strategy with Hans Wilhelm's book, *Bunny Trouble*.

PROBABLE PASSAGES: PREPARATION STAGE

Key Words

rabbit colony	Easter	decorating	deliver	design	soccer-crazy
nuisance	worried	Ralph	trouble	plan	promise
cage	free				

Story Frame

Setting	Beginning	Problem	Attempt	Outcome	Ending

Blank Probable Passage for _____

The story takes place _____
[setting]

_____ is a character in the story

who _____.
[beginning]

A problem occurs when _____
[problem]

_____

Then, _____
[attempt]

_____

The problem is solved when _____
[outcome]

_____

The story ends _____
[ending]

_____

Figure 3.4a The preparation stage for Probable Passages was completed by the teacher.

1. Preparation stage. The teacher wrote the key words, the story frame, and a blank probable passage on the whiteboard (see figure 3.4a).

2. Pre-reading stage. The teacher read the key words aloud, asking the students to repeat the words after her. She explained the meanings of terms and words that the students were unfamiliar with, such as *rabbit colony* and *nuisance*. She then said, "Think about these words, and see if you can come up with a story in your mind using as many of the words as you can." Next, she drew the students' attention to the story frame and reviewed the major elements in narrative or story structure. She asked students to place the key words into the appropriate places in the story frame. Then, she had them write the words, as they had already been organized in the story frame, to complete a logical Probable Passage (see figure 3.4b).

PROBABLE PASSAGES: PRE-READING STAGE

Setting	Beginning	Problem	Attempt	Outcome	Ending
rabbit colony	Easter decorating design Ralph soccer-crazy	trouble nuisance	deliver plan	worried cage	free promise

Probable Passage for ___Bunny Trouble___

The story takes place ___in a rabbit colony___. ___Ralph___ is a character in the story who ___is soccer-crazy.___. A problem occurs when ___it is Easter time and the rabbits have to decorate eggs___.

Then, ___Ralph gets into trouble. He gets kidnapped while he is playing soccer and somebody gets him and puts him in a cage___.

The problem is solved when ___Ralph gets his friends to help him break out of the cage___.

The story ends ___with Ralph promising never to play soccer again___.

Figure 3.4b The teacher helped her students use many of the words from the story frame to complete the probable passage.

3. Reading stage. The teacher directed the students, "Read this story. How does the story compare with how you thought the story might be?"

4. Post-reading stage. The teacher asked, "How did the actual story compare with your prediction?" The students agreed their probable passage was very close to the actual story. Finally, the teacher asked them to complete a blank Probable Passage, using the actual story (see figure 3.4c).

PROBABLE PASSAGES: POST-READING STAGE

Name: **Nicole**   Date: **January 20**

Theme: **Bunny Trouble**

Revised Probable Passage

The story takes place **in a rabbit colony in a forest**.

Ralph is a character in the story who **only cares about soccer and doesn't help the other bunnies decorate the eggs for Easter**.

A problem occurs when **Ralph goes off to play soccer by himself on the other side of the forest. A farmer catches him, puts him in a cage and is going to make him be Easter dinner**.

Then **everyone in the rabbit colony is worried about him and his mother cries**.

The problem is solved when **his sister Liza squeezes a basket of beautiful eggs into his cage. The farmer's children guess Ralph must be the Easter bunny and beg their father to let him go**.

The story ends **with Ralph running home. He still plays soccer but now he also helps the other bunnies**.

See BLM 3 in appendix for reproducible master.

Figure 3.4c When Probable Passages is used with older children, they can fill in their own activity sheet.

Related Information

Wood (Ibid.) recommends that after guiding students through several Probable Passages, you should encourage them to work in small cooperative groups to create their own Probable Passages. The small groups can then share their predictive stories with the rest of the class and decide for themselves, after reading the story, which groups' passages were closest to the actual story. Similarly, the revised Probable Passages can be composed in the same small groups and shared with the class as a whole.

CHAPTER 4
Teacher Questioning Strategies for Intermediate Grades

Students in the intermediate grades are busy exploring new ideas about themselves and the world around them. When the "right" questions are asked of them, they often amaze their teachers with their zealous intellectual curiosity. When we depart from simple factual recall and begin asking children what they think, feel, and believe, the classroom atmosphere becomes palpably "charged," and is an exciting place to be. The questioning activities in this chapter are appropriate for students who have some clearly developed writing skills, those who have had practice with the type of critical – and creative – thinking required by the activities in chapter 3, and/or for primary-age children who are eager for a more potent intellectual challenge.

THINK ALOUD

Rationale

Think Aloud is one of the most effective ways for a teacher to model critical questioning. This strategy shows, specifically, how a proficient reader uses a variety of reading skills to construct meaning from text. In addition to knowing about particular reading strategies, readers need to know when and why the strategies work. Teachers model all of these skills in Think Aloud as they show students what they do as they read.

When students learn to control and guide their reading, they are much more likely to become proficient readers (Baker and Brown 1984).

Description

The Think Aloud strategy was developed by Davey (1983). With this strategy, you read a passage aloud, and, at the same time, give the students an opportunity to hear you verbalize your thoughts – making comments and asking the kinds of probing questions that fluent readers use to derive meaning. Davey offers five techniques proficient readers use for thinking critically and processing the text:

1. Hypothesizing and predicting
2. Organizing images
3. Using prior knowledge
4. Monitoring one's own understanding
5. Rectifying comprehension errors

You can model Think Aloud in the following way:

1. Beforehand, make copies of the text passage you will demonstrate with or prepare to display the copy so that students can follow along. Explain to students that as they follow what you read, you will "think aloud" so that they can hear your thoughts.

2. Read the passage aloud while the students follow along. (The passage should be somewhat difficult for the students, with concepts and vocabulary slightly above the reading level of the learners.)

3. As you read aloud, talk through what strategy(ies) you are using to figure out vocabulary through the context, to decipher obscure phrases, or to relate the ideas in the text with those with which you are familiar.

4. After modeling several paragraphs, invite the students to add their own problem-solving tactics and personal impressions to your thought processes.

After you have modeled Think Aloud several times, provide students with short passages of similar difficulty. Encourage them to try the Think Aloud strategy with partners, rotating the oral reading and taking turns adding to the other person's thinking process. As students become adept at thinking aloud with partners, give them opportunities to read selected passages individually and to practice the newly learned thinking skills silently.

So that the students focus on the appropriate thinking procedures when they are using the strategy silently, have them ask themselves the following questions:

1. After looking at the cover, the title, and the pictures (if any) in this passage, what do I think it is going to be about? [hypothesizing and predicting]

2. What is going on right now in the passage? (to be asked at least after every paragraph) [organizing images]

3. What am I reminded of here that I already know about? [using prior knowledge]

4. What do I think these unfamiliar words might mean? What are some ways I can get clues to their meaning? [monitoring one's own understanding]

5. Do I want to change any of my original thinking as I read? (to be asked after every paragraph) [rectifying comprehension errors]

Example

The teacher read aloud a paragraph about lemmings from a passage entitled "The Mystery of the Lemmings." It tells about the lemmings' strange rush to the sea, which results in their drowning, and then asks why the animals would exhibit this behavior. These are the strategies modeled by the teacher as she read the passage aloud:

1. Hypothesizing. "'The Mystery of the Lemmings.' Hmmm. I really like mysteries, and they usually have some unsolved puzzle in them. I know that lemmings are small animals. I wonder what could be mysterious about them? Maybe they have some strange habits, like ostriches that bury their heads in the sand, or chameleons that change color."

2. Organizing images. "As I read along, I see that these little animals rush to the sea and drown! At first, I thought they must be running away to seek better feeding grounds, but it's not that because it says they pass by many of the things that they like to eat. I'm getting the idea that they don't know why they are going."

3. Using prior knowledge. "The description of the animals being about five inches long and with light brown fur reminds me of hamsters, or maybe gerbils. Probably lemmings are in the rodent family, although it doesn't say that."

4. Monitoring understanding. "As I read along, I'm changing what I first thought about why these animals drown themselves. I have confirmed what I thought – it's not for food – but I think maybe they do know why. I realized when it says that some stay back to start a family that not all of them go. Maybe it's like bees, in that certain lemmings have certain tasks, and they just seem to know what those tasks are."

5. Rectifying errors. "The first picture in my mind when it mentioned that lemmings drown themselves in the sea was some kind of starving, unhappy colony of animals that didn't want to live anymore. Then I began to think maybe they are like sheep and just followed the first one blindly. I'm changing my mind about that because of new information about feeding grounds and some lemmings staying behind. I think now that maybe these animals march to the sea for much the same reason that birds fly south for the winter – I have read that some inner clock or *instinct* is why birds fly south. Perhaps the same instinct is what makes the lemmings rush to the sea."

After you have modeled Think Aloud several times in various curricular areas, encourage students to crystallize their own Think Aloud questions and monitoring strategies, using an activity sheet (see figure 4.1). (The activity sheet should be phased out as the students internalize the strategy.)

THINK ALOUD	

Name:_____ Date: _____

Story Title: _____

1. How often did I ask myself what I thought this story or photograph was about?

    never   sometimes   often   after every paragraph

2. How often did I see pictures in my mind of what was going on?

    never   sometimes   often   after every paragraph

3. How often did what I read remind me of something else that I know about?

    never   sometimes   often   after every paragraph

4. How often did I stop to see if I was understanding what was going on in the story or paragraph?

    never   sometimes   often   after every paragraph

5. How often did I change what I had originally thought about what was going on in the story or passage?

    never   sometimes   often   after every paragraph

See BLM 4 in appendix for reproducible master.

Figure 4.1 Students can use the Think Aloud activity sheet until they learn the strategy.

INDUCTIVE REASONING

Rationale

Students are often asked to conduct research by gathering information from a variety of sources and then to make sense of a large collection of data. This can be a messy and daunting task. The Inductive Reasoning strategy provides steps and processes to help students make sense of their research. When students first use this model, the teacher may suggest categories for them by providing scaffolding and direction. As the students become familiar with the strategy and processes, they become more independent and construct their own questions and categories (Joyce and Weil 2004, based on Taba 1967).

Description

There are three parts to the Inductive Reasoning strategy:

1. Forming concepts: list, group, and label items
2. Interpreting data: identify and explore relationships, and draw inferences
3. Forming generalizations: predict, explain, and support consequences

Example

Students in this intermediate grade were studying the settlement of the United States. They began their study with a whole-class activity – creating a map to identify three regions, defining the geography of each area, and identifying the natural resources of the areas. They also began a class timeline that each group would add to throughout the unit of study.

The teacher then divided the class into three groups, one for each region of study.

Forming Concepts

The teacher had each group focus on collecting information for its region of study. Because this was the first time the class was using this strategy, the teacher created the categories and provided the students with scaffolding and direction. The teacher posted a chart on the whiteboard, and students from the three groups filled in the information to share with the rest of the class (see figure 4.2).

	Southern Colonies	Middle Colonies	New England Colonies
Present-day states	Georgia, North Carolina, South Carolina, Virginia, Maryland	New Jersey, Pennsylvania, New York, Delaware	Rhode Island, Connecticut, Massachusetts, New Hampshire
Who settled here?	English	Dutch	Puritans from Great Britain
What were their purposes?	Looking for gold, natural resources	Enrich Dutch stockholders	Freedom from religious persecution
What type of work did people typically do?	Farmers: cotton, tobacco, rice, sugar cane, indigo	Farmers, shipbuilders, paper and textile mills, ironworks	Farmers, fishers
What rewards did they realize?	Supplier of raw materials to England and northern colonies	Good farmland	Excellent harbors, religious freedom
What challenges did they have?	Not enough help to raise crops	Men often came without families; difficult without support	Poor soil, cold winters
How would you describe the values?	Family	Religious tolerance, compromise	Religious freedom, but did not always extend to others
How did people meet their basic needs (food, clothing, shelter)?	Shelters were large plantations	Shelters were farm houses away from villages and towns	Shelters were wooden houses

Figure 4.2 Students in this intermediate grade filled in the activity sheet created by their teacher.

Interpreting Data

After the chart (figure 4.2) was completed, the teacher engaged the students in a whole-class discussion of the data they had collected.

TEACHER: How would you describe each of the colonies?

PAM: The New England colonies were defined mostly by their pursuit of religious freedom. They did not have as many natural land resources, so they depended on the sea and on shipping.

HARRY: The Middle colonies were made up of large groups of people from different parts of Europe. They tolerated many different types of religious beliefs.

BETHANY: The Southern colonies were defined by the crops they could grow and the large plantations that developed.

TEACHER: How did the geography of each area affect how people met their basic needs?

CHARLES: The weather and the quality of the soil affected the food they could grow and what they could trade. The Southern colonies were almost completely dependent upon crops. The other colonies had other resources.

TEACHER: How did the type of work differ for each of the colonies?

ETHAN: The work depended on the resources and was closely related to the geography of the area.

TEACHER: Who can give me some specific examples?

NANCY: Fishing in the New England colonies developed because of the sea and rivers and the poor soil.

TEACHER: What were the causes of the challenges and rewards of each colony?

PALO: Sometimes the challenges and rewards came from the geography, but sometimes they came from their religious beliefs and values.

TEACHER: What role did religion play in the settlement of the different colonies?

BRENDA: Religion had a major role in New England and defined many of the communities and their laws. Religion was viewed differently in the Middle colonies. They had groups of people coming from different countries with different beliefs and practices.

Forming Generalizations

The teacher then engaged the students in a general discussion of the area of study.

TEACHER: Look at the timeline we created. Were there crucial turning points for the colonies? In other words, would their historical stories be different had some events not occurred or had occurred differently?

NANCY: The beginning events of each area seem to define later events.

TEACHER: If you were going to study other communities, what type of information would you collect to help you understand them?

DAVID: I think it is useful to know about the geography and the resources of an area. It is also nice to know about the daily lives of the people who live there and the work they do.

MARILYN: I would like to know what they do for fun. What did the children do? What games did they play?

TEACHER: I noticed that you used some information that was not on the chart to answer our discussion questions. Now that you have heard some of the ideas from other groups, you can go back and add information, generate some of your own questions, and answer the questions.

QUESTION-ELICITING QUESTIONS

Rationale

Singer's (1978) strategy for promoting self-questioning emanates from a modeling strategy that teachers may use to encourage children to ask questions, thus setting their own purposes for reading. Singer postulates that when students, not teachers, set the purposes for reading, they become more engaged in the search for answers. When self-questioning strategies are consistently used, children internalize the strategies and begin to construct text the way proficient readers do.

Description

Singer outlines three components for guiding comprehension through questions: (1) modeling, (2) phase-in/phase-out, and (3) critical thinking.

1. Modeling. Ask questions to determine what the students want to know.
2. Phase-in/phase-out. After modeling appropriate questions, write the questions students have about the text on the whiteboard. At this stage, you are phasing out your role as questioner and phasing in the students.
3. Critical thinking. Through your guidance, students learn to ask critical-thinking questions about the text in order to construct their own meanings.

Example

The teacher held up the book *Earl's Too Cool for Me*, by Leah Komaiko, and read the title aloud. Then she asked her first question-eliciting question, What do you want to know after hearing just the title of this book? Students responded with several questions, which the teacher duly recorded on the whiteboard:

- What does Earl do that is cool?
- Who is Earl?
- Who is telling the story about Earl?

- Is Earl an animal or a human?
- How old is Earl?

The teacher then read the first three lines of the story aloud:

> Earl's got a bicycle made of hay. He takes rides on the Milky Way. Earl's Too Cool for me.

The teacher asked a second question, "What would you like to know about Earl now?" The students responded with the following:

- Is Earl real?
- Is the person telling the story making it up?
- Does Earl ever get hurt?
- What else does Earl do?
- Is Earl a nice person?

The teacher then asked, "Is there anything you would like to ask the author of this story?" (The questions you ask, of course, depend on the content of the story.) The students responded with:

- What happens next?
- What else does Earl do that is cool?
- Where did the author get the idea for this story?
- Why did she choose this title?
- Does she think Earl is cool?
- Does the author like "cool" people?

METACOGNITION

Rationale

A major purpose of education is to have students "learn how to learn." It is impossible to teach students everything they need to know during their years of compulsory education. Thus, students must leave their public education experience with specific knowledge but also with the ability to continue learning for the rest of their lives. The Metacognition strategy shows students how to "think about their thinking." The emphasis is not on what to think but on how to think. With this knowledge, students have the ability to think through problems on their own. The strategy used in Metacognition allows students to become independent thinkers and learners (Ritchhart, Turner, and Hadar 2009).

Description

Re-introduce students to the thinking process chart in chapter 1 (see page 10). At the same time, give students inquiry- or problem-based projects to work on. After a few sessions, ask them the following questions:

- What kinds of thinking have you used to help you start to understand and solve your problem?
- Did you have any "dead-ends" – that is, you thought you were working in the right direction but needed to abandoned that route? What helped you come to this realization? What did you need to do to start working in a different direction?
- If you were to work on a different problem, what would you do the same?

As students continue to work on their projects, have a debriefing session every few days. These sessions give them opportunities to reflect on their overall progress and to discuss the processes and strategies that they are using. Students may also find it helpful to discuss their feelings, beliefs, and attitudes during these sessions. You can encourage them by asking questions such as the following:

- What new processes and strategies have you used in the last few days?
- Have you learned some new ways of acquiring data?
- Have you learned some new ways of organizing and making sense of your information?
- How does it make you feel to try new directions, new methods?

Continue to debrief students every few days during the project. A bulletin board may make their strategies and processes explicit and help them see how they use different processes at different times and refine processes as they apply them to new situations. At the end of the project, ask students the following questions:

- If I were to have students work on this next year, what advice or guidelines would you give them?
- What kinds of ideas will you remember to apply to the next project that we work on?
- What kinds of feelings did you have to work with?

Example

Students were working on a nomination of new animals for the local zoo. At first, the students enthusiastically listed many animals from all over the world. They had many more ideas for animals than could be added to the zoo. They soon found that they were at an impasse.

TEACHER: What have we done so far?

ANNA: We have brainstormed a list of different animals.

TEACHER: Does anyone have an idea about what we could do to progress from making a list of animals to making some specific suggestions to the zoo?

ZACK: We could categorize the animals.

JUAN: We could research more specific information about the animals that are already at the zoo and the animals that we are suggesting.

TEACHER: Okay, let's spend the next couple of days thinking about what we have talked about.

A few days later, the students and teacher continued their discussion.

TEACHER: What kinds of thinking have you used in the last few days?

KEZIAH: To create categories, we had to find out where the animals usually live, what their basic needs are, who their prey are, and who might prey on them.

TEACHER: How did you feel about doing all of this?

ILYA: At first, I think we were frustrated and irritated with each other. As we started to think about what information we didn't have, we began to get new ideas. We then began searching for different information.

TEACHER: What do you think should be the basis for suggesting animals for the zoo?

ANNA: At first, I thought if people did not like the animal I suggested, they might not like me. Now that we have more information, there are some different reasons for choosing.

At the end of the project, the teacher and students had this discussion:

TEACHER: What thinking processes did you use for this project?

ZACK: We used categorizing, sequencing, and analyzing.

TEACHER: What advice would you give to students who were about to work on a similar project?

KEZIAH: I would say to have a plan that goes beyond gathering information. Think about how to sort and organize your information.

TEACHER: What did you learn about feelings and attitudes?

ILYA: Sometimes you have to take a point of view that is different from the view you had at the beginning. You have to be flexible.

CAMILA: You can't jump to conclusions before you have enough information. You have to listen to and respect the ideas of other people.

EXPERIENCE-TEXT RELATIONSHIP

Rationale

Students cannot always relate their experiences to a topic before reading. Their backgrounds must be brought to bear at all phases of the reading process through effective teacher questioning. Au has had great success helping diverse learners achieve in reading by making the past experiences of each child an integral part of the entire lesson. In Au's Experience-Text Relationship (ETR) strategy (Au 1979; Cecil 1993), students practice expressing complex thoughts. As they respond to questions, the teacher gets an idea about which steps are easy or difficult for individual students. Through the teacher's questioning, cuing, and prompting, the students are able to integrate features of the new story with their existing understandings of the world. Students who have interacted frequently with a teacher in ETR are better able to think critically than those who have not been afforded this opportunity.

Description

Au's critical-thinking lessons are composed of three different kinds of sequences: (1) an experience sequence for eliciting background; (2) a text sequence for determining what meaning the children are deriving from the material; and (3) a relationship sequence, in which children compare their own experiences with what they have just read. The lesson proceeds as follows:

1. Experience. Ask students questions about experiences they have had, or ask them to share certain knowledge they have that is directly related to the story they will soon read or hear.

2. Text. After all students have had an opportunity to share their knowledge or experiences, have them read or listen to short passages from the story (usually a page or two at a time), asking them critical-thinking questions about the content after each section is read. If their responses reveal misunderstandings due to their differing world views, you must then add the necessary background information to correct the misunderstandings.

3. Relationship. At this point, attempt to make connections for the students between the content of the story, as discussed in the text sequence (#2, above), and their own outside experiences and knowledge, as shared in the experience sequence (#1, above).

Example

A fourth-grade teacher guided her students through an ETR sequence, incorporating Jay William's book, *The Practical Princess*, about an unorthodox princess with a good deal of common sense. The teacher, concerned that the author's clever use of satire may be misinterpreted by the students, felt ETR (because of its constant questioning) was the best strategy to help students better appreciate the story.

Experience

Before reading the story, the teacher asked the students to share experiences and knowledge they thought might relate to the story they were about to read.

> **TEACHER:** Do any of you know what it means to be practical? Can you give me an example of someone, or something, you or someone else has done that could be considered practical?

NICOLE: Well, once my sister asked my mother if she would like a mink coat for her birthday. I remember she answered that she already had a coat, and a microwave oven would be more practical.

RAUL: I went camping one time, and my uncle said to wear practical shoes. He meant, I think, not my Sunday-best ones, just sturdy ones.

TEACHER: Those are both very good examples. Nicole, your mother wanted a microwave oven because she would use it more. It would be more sensible for her than a mink coat. Raul, you were advised to wear practical shoes – not fancy ones that wouldn't be sensible. Now, I'd like us to read a story about a princess who is not like some of the princesses you may have read about. She is not always concerned with fine jewelry and clothes; instead, she is constantly using her head to get out of bad situations. Let's find out what she does that makes her seem so practical.

Text

As the students read several paragraphs at a time, the teacher stopped them periodically to discuss the text. By probing the students' thinking as they were reading, the teacher tried to clear up any misunderstandings and modeled how a proficient reader can think through confusing parts.

TEACHER: Why do you think the princess says to the dragon that he only wants to marry her because he's a snob?

RANA: Who would want to marry a dragon? She's probably waiting for Prince Charming. (*Other children laugh.*)

TEACHER: Well, that's what happens in lots of fairy tales, isn't it, Rana? But it might be that this princess has another reason for not wanting to get married. Does the dragon really love the princess, do you think?

NICOLE: Uh-uh. He just thinks he has to marry a princess because princesses are supposed to be so cool! That's why she thinks the dragon is a snob. He just cares too much what other people think.

TEACHER: Good thinking, Nicole. He doesn't care at all what she is like as long as she's a princess. How do you feel about this kind of thinking?

Relationship

Having cleared up several confusions similar to the one cited in the previous sequence, the teacher was now confident that the children had gained a fuller appreciation of the tale. She was ready to relate the story with the students' prior experiences and knowledge.

TEACHER: Have you ever known anyone who used her head to get out of bad experiences the way Princess Bedelia did?

RANA: Yeah, the woman in *Alien II*. She led everyone to safety using her smarts (*Others laugh.*). Princesses are usually too busy being beautiful to use their brains. It was cool the way Princess Bedelia did, though. She could have just gone along with it and married the dragon the way everyone expected her to.

TEACHER: Yes – that is what we have come to expect in fairy tales, isn't it? How did you like how she managed to keep from marrying the dragon?

NICOLE: That was really cool. She got him to come out of the cave by telling him to come and get her, and then she blew him up. Kerpow! That's sort of like how I trick my dog to get him to take a bath. He hides under the bed when he sees the hose, so I bribe him with a dog biscuit. (*Others laugh.*)

RANA: It sounds like you use your common sense to get your dog into the bathtub!

TEACHER: Yes! I guess Nicole is practical sometimes too, right?

SCAMPERing

Rationale

This strategy, devised by Eberle (1984), helps students understand how to generate new ideas by linking them with existing ones. SCAMPERing is useful as a pre-writing questioning strategy when it is used in conjunction with any story from a basal reader or trade book. It can also be used as an enrichment tool for increasing the flexibility of students' thinking about stories and improving their divergent thinking skills. If students are engaged in problem solving and decision making, this strategy can help them think of new ways to address situations.

Description

SCAMPER is an acronym that describes the quest for ideas and images about stories that have previously been read. Each letter in the word is the first letter of the name of a creative-thinking technique included in the process: Substitute, Combine, Adapt, Modify/Magnify, Put to Use/Point of View, Eliminate, Rearrange/Reverse. These techniques generate thought-provoking questions to create exciting new stories.

1. Substitute. What item or event in the story can be changed to another item or event? How would this substitution change the whole story?

2. Combine. What characters from other stories would you like to add to this one to change the events in the story? How will the story turn out now?

3. Adapt. How could the results of one conversation or event lead to a different ending to this story?

4. Modify. What event can be changed so that the story has a different ending?

5. Magnify. What will happen to the characters after the story has ended?

6. Put to use. How can you give a character more to do or say in the story, or how can some item be used more than it was?

7. Point of view. How would the story be different if it were told by one of the other characters?

8. Eliminate. What would happen if you got rid of one of the main characters in the story?

9. Rearrange. Change the order of events in this story. How will this affect the ending?

10. Reverse. Give the main characters the opposite personality traits. How will the story be different if the good characters become bad, and the bad characters become good?

Example

A teacher used the SCAMPERing strategy to help students think about the book, *The Three Billy Goats Gruff*, by P. C. Asbjornsen, in fresh and original ways – through thought-provoking questions that culminated in written responses.

Substitute

Substitute one item in the story for another. What might have happened if the billy goats had had to go through a tunnel instead of cross a bridge?

Combine

Combine characters from the story or from another story, and compare them and revise the story accordingly. What would happen if the three goats joined forces with the three little pigs?

Adapt

Make an adaptation of a character's behavior or of a plot feature. What might have happened if all three billy goats had attempted to cross the bridge at the same time?

Modify

Change or modify an element of the plot. What do you think the troll might have done if the goats had made no noise crossing the bridge?

Magnify

Extend the story. What do you think will happen in the goats' lives, now that they are safely on the other side of the bridge?

Put to Use

Intensify the role of some element or character in the story. In what other ways might the goats have used their horns?

Point of View

Rewrite the story from the point of view of a different character. How would the story be different through the eyes of the troll?

SCAMPERing

Name: **Greta**   Date: **January 8**

Theme: **The Three Little Pig**

To rewrite the story in a new way, select a question, then answer in the space at the bottom (turn the page if you need more room).

1. Substitute: What might have happened if the three little pigs had been camping rather than living in houses?

2. Combine: What would happen if Little Red Riding Hood and the wolf joined the three little pigs?

3. Adapt: What might have happened if the police had come?

4. Modify: What would happen if the wolf could not blow?

5. Magnify: How might the story end if the wolf had not eaten the first two pigs?

6. Put to Use: What other abilities could the wolf have had that the pigs would have had to pay attention to?

7. Point of View: How would the story be different if the wolf was kind and the pigs were mean?

8. Eliminate: How would the lives of the pigs be different if the wolf had never come along?

9. Rearrange: How would the story be different if the pigs had met the wolf at a friend's house?

10. Reverse: How would the story be different if the wolf had gone to the brick house first?

Answer: ____ Magnify. The last we saw the wolf, he was running away, and the pigs were jumping up and down with joy. Oscar felt proud that he had outwitted the wolf and saved his friends. The first two pigs, James and Freddy, asked to live in the brick house with him, because Mr. Wolf had completely destroyed their houses. So they moved in. They had a big party and invited all of their friends. Things were great for a while. Then Oscar started to get really annoyed that he was the only one cleaning up after himself. He gave James and Freddy three warnings, but they would never help. So finally Oscar kicked them out. For three weeks they were homeless. Then they got an idea. They went to Oscar's house one night, pretending to be a wolf. With both of them huffing and puffing, they really sounded just like the wolf. Oscar freaked. He started running around shouting, "James! Freddy! Help! I'm in trouble!" Freddy and James flung open the door and yelled, "It's just us!" At first Oscar was mad, but then he got over it. He was so relieved to not see the wolf that he told James and Freddy they could stay. They promised they would help clean up. As far as I know, all three pigs are still living together.

Figure 4.3 A student uses the SCAMPERing activity sheet to help her create a new version of *The Three Little Pigs.*

See BLM 5 in appendix for reproducible master.

Eliminate

Get rid of one of the major characters. How would the story be different if there were no troll?

Rearrange

Change the sequence of events. Imagine that the largest billy goat had crossed the bridge first. How would the ending of the story change?

Reverse

Switch the prominent personality characteristics of the main characters. How would you rewrite the story if the peace-loving troll was trying to cross the bridge, but the three irritable goats would not let him?

FICTIONAL ROLE-PLAYS

Rationale

Proficient readers infuse intellectual and emotional meanings into text. The particular definitions and associations the words in a book have for each reader determine exactly what the message communicates to him or her and greatly enhance the meaning of text and the enjoyment of reading. Thus, it is important for the teacher to foster such "fruitful transactions" between the student-reader and the text. One way to do this is to provide a strategy in which students are invited to respond in a personal way to characters in children's literature. Fictional Role-Plays is such a strategy. Children are asked to become the characters, while their classmates ask them probing questions about their behaviors and motivations.

Role-playing can also help students solve real-life problems (for example, in the playground). In addition, role-playing allows them to consider historical events from multiple points of view. Students can role-play an historical event as it actually occurred, and then "rewrite" history by predicting different behaviors and, therefore, different outcomes. Students might act out different scenarios and discuss the advantages and disadvantages of various options.

Description

When reading a book with many complex characters to a group of young children, Fictional Role-Plays can help make the characters in the book come alive. Through interactive questioning, students can discover the relationship between what they are reading and their own lives (Cecil 1994). Use the procedure for Fictional Role-Plays as follows:

1. In collaboration with the students, decide on a piece of literature to role-play. Fairly lengthy works with many three-dimensional characters work best.

2. As a class, write a list on the whiteboard of all the characters in the book.

3. Assign a pair of students to each character.

4. Have students reread the story, this time to get to know their own character better.

5. Have each student pair draw up a list of critical questions for other characters in the book. Such questions might be those that a reader longs to ask a character, or they can be posed character to character. Also, encourage students to ask probing questions that go beyond the scope of the book.

6. After this preparation has been completed, the students are ready for the role-playing. Have each pair wear a character name tag so classmates can identify the character they wish to question, then have all sit in a circle.

7. Open the session by asking a question to a pair of characters, modeling the strategy. If the answer is offered superficially or with a simple yes or no response, then demonstrate to students how to probe to get the character to elaborate.

8. Have the students go around the circle, asking a question of a different character each time. Encourage other students to ask follow-up questions to each question, such as, Could you tell me more about that? or Why did you think so?

Example

A class of sixth-grade students decided to do Fictional Role-Play with the story *Peter Pan*, by J. M. Barrie, after reading the book and watching the video in class. To start, the teacher, with the students' help, made a list of characters from the book and assigned roles to pairs of children.

Characters:

Author	Wendy	John
Captain Hook	Lost Boy (1)	Tinker Bell
Mr. Darling	Pirate (1)	Crocodile (Tick Tocks)
Mrs. Darling	Nana (dog)	Indian Princess
Peter Pan	Michael	Mr. Smee

The students reviewed the story in light of their own character and created questions they wanted to ask other characters in the book. The following day, students sat in a circle with their name tags around their necks and asked questions.

STUDENT: Peter Pan, do you ever see Wendy now that she has grown up?

PETER PAN: Yes, I stop in every once in a while to see how she's doing. She's not any fun anymore, though. She has two children of her own, and she's a secretary. She's not interested in flying around anymore.

STUDENT: Pirate, what do you think your punishment might have been if you had been caught trying to make people walk the plank?

PIRATE: Gosh, I wasn't thinking about punishment! I was just having fun! I bet they would give me life imprisonment unless I pleaded insanity. I think I would get away with it, too, because nobody else I know does anything as cruel as making people jump into water with a crocodile. Maybe I *am* crazy!

STUDENT: Mrs. Darling, how did you feel when you first learned that your children were gone from the nursery?

MRS. DARLING: Well, I was very upset, of course.

ANOTHER STUDENT: If you were so upset about losing your children, Mrs. Darling, why didn't you call the FBI or something?

STUDENT: Peter Pan, can you explain why it is that you don't want to grow up?

PETER PAN: When I'm a child, I can do just exactly what I want to do and fly around always having fun. If I don't grow up, I will never have to go out and get a job and pay bills and taxes.

Related Information

As illustrated, role-playing can help students comprehend stories and historical events. Role-playing can also help students solve problems in everyday life. For instance, students can role-play problems they encounter at the playground. If the class is trying to raise funds for a field trip or a charitable cause, students might role-play different people and situations that they might encounter. Some teachers have found it useful to identify situations in which students might experience peer pressure and have them use role-playing to generate ways of responding to the pressure.

PROMPTING

Rationale

Often when a teacher asks a question and a student has been selected to respond to it, that student will answer only part of the question, or none at all. Prompting is used when the teacher (1) needs to clarify the question so that the student can understand it better, (2) wants to encourage the student to amplify the response, or (3) wants to elicit additional responses from the student. Prompting enables the teacher to verify whether or not a student actually has a critical understanding of the material. Prompting also ensures that a student's sense of competence is not diminished by lack of success.

Description

The first rule: Always prompt in a positive manner. As you develop the strategy of prompting, there are many steps you can follow. Some are:

1. Acknowledge the student's response.
2. If the student has not answered a question correctly, prompt.
3. Ask for clarification or elaboration.
4. Respond positively to a correct or partially correct clarification.

5. Prompt the student to restate the answer more completely or more logically. If the student does so, offer him or her specific praise.

6. If the student is still unable to restate the answer more completely or logically, ask if another classmate can assist the student.

Example

In this fifth-grade classroom, the students had just read Katherine Paterson's *Bridge to Terabithia*. The teacher-guided discussion, which shows the teacher prompting Evelyn, went as follows:

TEACHER: Why did Jesse and Leslie become friends? It seemed to me very unlikely that the two would form a friendship. (*Waits.*) Evelyn?

EVELYN: Well – they liked to race each other.

TEACHER: Yes, they both enjoyed running, and that is how they first met. Exactly right! What other things did they enjoy doing together that made their friendship grow?

EVELYN: They swung on the rope across the river.

TEACHER: Okay – that's part of it. Now, what did they do when they got on the other side of the creek?

EVELYN: Well, they built Terabithia together. It was like their own special little place where they were the rulers, and neat things happened. They – they both liked using their imaginations. That's what Jesse liked about Leslie, the part about not feeling afraid to make stuff up.

TEACHER: Great! You really understood their friendship! Now, how about going back to summarize what you discovered about the reasons for their friendship?

CHAPTER 5
Student Questioning Strategies for Primary Grades

The most exciting times in teaching occur, many teachers would agree, when students are so interested and involved in a subject that the questions emanate from them. They are no longer just pleasing the teacher; they are asking questions of themselves, of the teacher, and of each other – merely for the joy of learning.

If asking appropriate questions is difficult for teachers, it is also a lofty task for students. Beginning as early as in the primary grades, however, children can be taught to ask their own questions by using activities such as the ones in this chapter. The activities are also appropriate for older students as the difficulty of the content increases.

SELF-INSTRUCTION

Rationale

Self-Instruction helps learners become aware of their own cognitive processes through self-questioning (McNeil 1984). The assumption is that, if the student can connect the use of this strategy to particular gains in understanding, he or she will then use the strategy when the teacher is not around. The practice of asking students to state what they are doing and why they are doing it when they are learning any new strategy is one way to help them make the connection between self-questioning and actual learning.

Description

Self-Instruction is actually a combination of three metacognitive strategies. Self-interrogation, verbal monitoring, and thinking aloud all help learners become aware of their own thinking. A student who uses Self-Instruction does the following:

- Defines the problem (What do I have to do?)
- Focuses attention (What is the main idea in this paragraph?)
- Plans an action (The main idea is a summary of the most important ideas in a piece of writing. I will look for a sentence that sums up what this paragraph is all about.)
- Evaluates (Have I found it yet?)
- Encourages self (That's all right. I'll keep trying.)
- Revises (Could the main idea be in more than one sentence?)
- Copes (I'll try this new plan.)

When you teach Self-Instruction strategy, you first model, talking aloud to the students while you demonstrate a particular reading task (for example, drawing conclusions, determining the topic sentence).

Then, the students "rehearse" the strategy you have shown them by telling what they are doing as they are doing it (see statements and self-questions above). These rehearsals aloud are followed by silent rehearsals: Students attack a reading task by using Self-Instruction independently, then reporting on their strategies. Finally, students practice by using the reading task on their own with a variety of other materials. The same procedure – modeling, rehearsing aloud, silent rehearsing, practicing with other reading material – is carried out with other reading tasks, such as finding supporting evidence for a generalization, locating specific information, or inferring mood. In every case, the components of problem definition – focus, plan of action, evaluation, encouragement, revision, and coping, as necessary – should be present.

Example

After reading the following paragraphs, a second-grade student used Self-Instruction to choose a title for a passage about veterinarians.

> What kind of person would be a good vet? It's important to do well in school, but you need more than good grades to be a good vet. You must like animals and care about helping them when they are sick.

> You have to look carefully – watch your patient's behavior to figure out what it may be feeling. And you should enjoy working out puzzles. You'll have some of the pieces: the patient's temperature, the sound of its heart and lungs, the results of blood tests, how the eyes and ears look, and how the body feels, for example. Then you have to put all the information together to figure out what is wrong.

The student proceeded in the following way:

1. He defined the problem. Well, I have to make a title for this passage.
2. He focused attention. The title tells what the passage is going to be about.
3. He planned an action. If I can think of a few words that are found in most of the sentences in the paragraphs, it will probably make a good title.

4. He evaluated. How about "I Want to Be a Vet"? No, it doesn't tell about all that stuff about puzzles. I have to think of a better one.

5. He encouraged himself. That one wasn't good, but that's okay. I'll think of another one.

6. He revised. The second part is all about what you have to do to be a vet. How about "Becoming a Vet"?

7. He coped. "I'll look at all these sentences now and see if they go with "Becoming a Vet.""

QUESTION-ANSWER RELATIONSHIPS

Rationale

The three metacognitive processes necessary for proficient reading are: (1) self-knowledge (knowing one's own strengths and weaknesses in understanding text), (2) self-monitoring (being aware of whether or not comprehension is occurring), and (3) task knowledge (knowing what reading strategies are required by the particular reading material). Question-Answer Relationships (QARs) (Raphael 1982; Jones and Leahy 2006; Ouzts 1998), helps students discover for themselves whether the questions they are being asked are explicitly answered in the text or require more than one source of information (or divergent thinking) that is not totally based upon text information.

Description

When students use QARs for understanding how to answer specific questions, they learn the different tactics readers use to answer literal, inferential, critical, and creative questions. Specifically, the student asks, Where can I find an answer?, then uses the following hierarchy of questions and answers to decide:

- Question type 1 [literal]. Answer: Right there. This response tells the student that the answer is easy to find in the story. The exact words in the question are contained in the story.

- Question type 2 [inferential]. Answer: Think and search. This response tells the student that the answer can be found in the story, but he or she will have to put two ideas together – that is, the words used in the question may be a bit different from the words used in the story, so the answer will be harder to find.

- Question type 3 [critical]. Answer: The author and me. The answer is in the story, but there is only one way the question can be answered – from the author's point of view. The student may think of another way to answer the question after considering the author's ideas.

- Question type 4 [creative]. Answer: On my own. The student will not find the "exact" answer to this kind of question in the story. The answer may come from his or her imagination or from information he or she already knows about the topic.

The following outline shows how you can train your students to incorporate this helpful strategy into their reading and thinking.

- First session. Give students a passage with questions for which the question types have already been determined. Discuss with them how each question-and-answer relationship is decided. Then, give them a passage for which they must determine the type of question and find the answer in the passage.

- Second session. Provide students with longer passages of several paragraphs and with up to eight questions per passage. With your guidance, allow students to discuss the questions in small cooperative groups.

- Third session. Give students entire stories to read, divided into four sections. Provide eight questions, two from each category, for each section.

- Fourth session. Offer material from other curricular materials (for example, science and social studies) accompanied by two or three questions for each QARs' category. Instruct students to read the passage, respond to each question by identifying the QARs, and then discuss the answer.

Example

After reading an excerpt from C. J. Naden's book, *Pegasus the Winged Horse* (below), a group of third-graders used QARs to help them answer the four categories of questions.

> Long ago in Ancient Greece, there was a very special horse called Pegasus. He was special because he could fly. Pegasus had great snowy wings that lifted him right into the clouds. Sometimes he played games in the clouds, gliding from one to another like a big white bird. Everyone on earth loved Pegasus because he was such a beautiful and gentle horse. And he was a favorite, too, with the gods and goddesses who lived high on Mount Olympus.

TEACHER: What made Pegasus special?

DION: "Right there." He was special because he could fly.

TEACHER: What did Pegasus do for fun?

DION: "Think and search," because it doesn't use those words exactly. He played games in the clouds.

TEACHER: Do you think Pegasus was very popular? Why?

DION: "Think and search." I would say he was very popular, because it says here that everyone on earth loved him, and he was also a favorite with the gods and goddesses.

TEACHER: Why do you think everyone liked Pegasus so much?

JENNIFER: "Think and search." It says that Pegasus was a beautiful and gentle horse. That's probably why everyone loved him so much.

SIM: "Author and me," I think. Being beautiful and gentle may have been part of it, but probably they loved him too because it was so unusual to see a horse that could fly.

TEACHER: Was he part of the earth or part of the sky?

DION: "Author and me." People on earth loved him and so did the gods and goddesses, but it's not really clear whether he was *part* of one or the other. I think he was probably more part of the sky because he enjoyed flying so much.

TEACHER: Would you like to own a horse that could fly? Why or why not?

JENNIFER: "On my own." This is definitely just my own opinion. I would love to have a winged horse that I could fly all over the world, especially a pretty, gentle horse.

SIM: Yeah, it's "on my own," because I have a different opinion. I really love horses, but I would prefer one that would just be normal and gallop around places. People would stare at you too much if you had a flying horse.

INTERVIEWING/SURVEYING

Rationale

Much of the information that young students use in school comes from books. However, students learn from other sources as well. This strategy engages students in the collection of information by having them interview or survey other people and then making sense of the information that they collect. Surveys are usually paper-based. Categories and trends can be determined from the information collected from large numbers of people. Interviews are usually conducted face-to-face, and they allow students to clarify answers and follow up for more detail immediately (http://library.ucsc.edu/reg-hist/oral-history-primer).

Description

Both surveys and interviews begin by generating questions that lead to data collection. The data invite students to compare, categorize, draw inferences, and investigate points of view. Oral histories are from a specific type of interview that allows the researcher to understand social history rather than the political history typically depicted in textbooks.

Before students conduct real interviews, have the students, in pairs, role-play the following steps:

1. Determine the focus of the interview/survey. Is it a general recollection or a specific topic?

   General recollection: For example, How would you describe what your childhood (at eight years of age) was like?

   Specific topic: For example, What tasks or chores did you have to do when you were eight years old?

2. Plan categories, and formulate questions for each topic. For example, if food was a category, a question to ask might be, What was your favorite food to eat when you were eight years old?

3. Rehearse or model the interview.

4. Let the person being interviewed know the general types of questions in advance (the purpose of the interview).

5. Arrange a time and place to hold the interview.

6. Bring along an adult to help with taking notes. Or record the interview to help you remember the answers to your questions.

7. At the interview, have an ice breaker (warm up the interviewee). Ask the interviewee questions that are not directly related to, but may lead into, the interview topic. For instance, How long have you lived in the area?

   Make sure the person you are interviewing is comfortable by asking, for example, Are you comfortable sitting where you are, or would you like to change seats?

   Be a good listener – and look at the person, make eye contact, smile, and nod at appropriate times, showing that you understand (use body language).

   - Try not to interrupt.
   - Ask your questions orally, or have the person you are interviewing fill out a form with the questions on it.
   - Ask easy questions first.
   - Ask one question at a time.
   - Ask follow-up questions for more details.
   - Ask for examples.
   - Say thank you, and show appreciation for the person's time and information.

8. Share what you found out with other class members.

9. Summarize what you learned.

Example

> TEACHER (*Presenting students with a focus.*): You want to find out how life has changed since your grandparents were the age you are today. What kinds of questions might you ask? Let's start by thinking about the things you do in the morning and during the day. (*Prompts when necessary.*)

Students gave the following responses, which the teacher wrote on the whiteboard:

- I get dressed the first thing in the morning.
- I eat breakfast before I go to school.
- I go to school from 8 to 2 every day.
- I make my bed before I go to school.
- I feed the dog before I leave home.

- I get an allowance of $1 a week. Sometimes, I stop at the store on my way to school.
- I spend recess time with my friends.
- I like to play games on the computer and play soccer.
- I sometimes forget to do my homework.

  TEACHER (*Prompting for more detail.*): Let's put your responses into categories and brainstorm specific questions we can ask for each of these categories.

Students generated categories and questions that they could use in the surveys and interviews.

Clothing

- What did you usually wear to school?
- What did you wear for special occasions?

Food

- What was your favorite food to eat?

School

- When did you go to school?

Chores

- What kinds of chores did you have?

Spending Money

- Did you get paid for doing your chores? How much?

Pets

- Did you have any pets? Who cared for them?

Friends

- What did you do with your friends?

Fun Activities

- What was your favorite thing to do with your free time?

Punishment

- Did you ever get into trouble? For what? What happened?

Family

- How many brothers and sisters did you have?

The teacher and a pre-selected student then modeled the interview/survey process in front of the class. The teacher wrote notes on the whiteboard for all students to see. She also read the questioning check-off sheet aloud.

TEACHER: Now, let's try to find out about ourselves and practice asking questions at the same time.

Student pairs modeled the process together. Students completed forms to request an interview with another student and conducted their interviews.

TEACHER: Now that you have had the chance to ask and answer the interview questions, do you think any questions need to be changed or reworded (for example, perhaps you found a question too difficult to answer)? Does the order of the interview questions need to be changed?

Following the interview rehearsals, the teacher created a class chart to summarize the interviewees' responses to each question. Figure 5.1 (below) shows the section of the chart that was filled out for the question, Did you have any pets?

Pet		Cat	Dog	Horse	Hamster	Snake	Fish	Bird	Other
Number	4+	✓	✓				✓		
	3							✓	
	2				✓				✓
	1			✓					

Figure 5.1 The teacher created a chart to summarize the students' responses to one of the interview questions.

When students were comfortable doing interviews in the classroom, they conducted real interviews with people outside the classroom. First, they sent out a request letter to the person they wanted to interview (see figure 5.2). Next, they wrote out the questions they wanted to ask – leaving space for recording the answers during the actual interview (see figure 5.3). Following the interviews, the teacher had each student complete an interview check-off form similar to figure 5.4. Students then compared their responses.

Dear Grandma,

My class is studying about the daily lives of 8-year-old children now and long ago. We have some questions that we are asking all of our grandparents or friends who are grandparent-age. We want to know about the clothing, food, chores, pets, and fun activities when you were eight. Would you be willing to answer some questions for me on Wednesday, January 30, at 7:00 p.m.? We can meet at your house.

Sincerely,

Misha

See BLM 6 in appendix for reproducible master.

Figure 5.2 A student invited her grandmother to participate in an interview. Requests for interviews/oral histories can be made by letter or by telephone.

My name: _____

Person interviewed: _____

I know this person because _____

Date and time of interview: _____

Question	Answer
What was your favorite food?	
What did you like to do for fun?	
Did you have any pets? Who took care of them?	
What was your favorite thing to do after school?	
What did you usually do for your birthday?	
What did you usually do with your friends?	
Did you have jobs or chores around the house? Did you get paid for them?	
If you got in trouble, what did you get in trouble for?	
What was your punishment?	

Figure 5.3 An example of an interview worksheet that was developed by a class to help organize questions and responses.

✓	Did I:
	Arrange an agreed-upon time and place for the interview?
	Share the purpose of the interview?
	Ask all of the questions I had planned to ask?
	Keep good eye contact and positive body language?
	Ask follow-up questions for more detail?
	Thank the person I was interviewing for his/her time and information?

Figure 5.4 Following their interviews, students fill out the Interview Check-Off Sheet.

Related Information

For more information on oral histories and creating surveys, check out the following resources:

- Samples of oral histories

    http://genealogy.about.com/od/oral_history/tp/stories_online.htm

    http://dohistory.org/on_your_own/toolkit/oralHistory.html#QUESTIONS

- Tutorial to help students design their own survey questionnaires

    http://www.mathsisfun.com/data/survey-questionnaire.html

BASAL READER PREDICTION

Rationale

Prior to reading, when students make predictions about what something is about, they have set their own purpose. They will then read to find out if their predictions are supported in the passage. Moreover, when students share and discuss their predictions, friendly arguments about whose predictions are correct often follow, adding even more impetus to the reading task (Tierney, Readence, and Dishner 1985). Buckley (1986) avows that writing can be used to help students develop elaborate predictions about the basal stories they are about to read.

Description

Pair students, or divide the class into small student groups, then do the following (basal reader stories or stories from trade books may be used):

1. Have the partners or members of the group leaf through, in order, all the illustrations in the story. Then, have each partner or group member select an illustration and carefully describe aloud to his or her partner or group what is happening in it.

2. After each illustration is described, have the next student in the pair or group predict aloud what will happen in that part of the story.

3. After all the illustrations in the story have been discussed, have each student write his or her own story predicting what will happen in the story, according to what was described in the illustrations.

4. Have partners or group members share their stories and discuss their opinions about the accuracy of each other's predictions.

5. Have the partners or group members take turns reading the story aloud or silently to check their predictions.

6. Have the partners or group members compare the story with their predictive stories and discuss who came closest to the actual story line.

Example

Two second-grade readers used the prediction strategy for the book *Puss in Boots* by S. Saunders. This is what happened. (Note: The process continued until all the illustrations had been discussed.)

Step 1

> LEON: In the first picture, it shows three men, and one of them has a cat in his arms. It looks like it is his cat, and he loves it a lot.
>
> MICAH: I think the other two men are going to try to take the cat away from the man. (*Pauses.*) My turn for the next picture. This is the same man 'cause he has the same clothes on, but he looks younger, like a boy. The cat is talking to him, and he looks surprised.
>
> LEON: I think the cat is telling the boy that he will take care of him.

Step 2

Leon and Micah wrote the following predictive stories based upon the discussions and predictions they made for each illustration:

Micah's Story

The cat who can talk gets all dressed up in fancy clothes. He meets a bad man and then a lion and a mouse. The cat makes the boy who owns him rich. He becomes a king and he still keeps his cat.

Leon's Story

The boy is afraid of his cat because he can talk. He tries to get rid of him. The cat puts on a costume and goes in the woods. He goes to see the king. The king tells him to bring the boy back, so he does.

Step 3

Leon and Micah shared their written stories with each other. Micah argued intensely that the boy still loved the cat. Leon did not think so but was less sure after discussion with Micah. Both agreed it was not a true story.

Step 4

The two young students read *Puss in Boots*.

Step 5

Leon and Micah had the following discussion:

LEON: Neither one of us got it that the cat could change himself into other animals.

MICAH: Yeah, but I was right about the boy still caring for the cat. The cat was a *good* cat, and I said that.

LEON: But I was right about the king. He [the cat] went to see the king. He was trying to get money for his master, who was poor.

MICAH: You were right in some ways, and I was right in some ways.

SEQUENCING

Rationale

Information on a topic often comes from several sources and in a variety of formats. When we prepare to use the information, we may find it difficult to remember and use these pieces of separate and seemingly unrelated pieces. Very seldom do we use information in the same form that we received it. Sequencing allows us to organize new information into patterns. With these patterns, we can add new information or search our memory to retrieve and use retained information.

Description

Sequencing information may involve listing the information in alphabetical order, numerical order (from large to small or vice versa), temporal order (minutes, hours, days, weeks, years), spatial order (closer or farther away), natural order or order of occurrence, or order of importance to the user. The same information can be ordered in different ways for different purposes. This activity becomes more complex if all of the information is not in equal increments.

Example

In this classroom, the teacher divided the class into five groups, then showed students the book *Miss Tizzy* by Libba Moore Gray. *Miss Tizzy* is a story about activities that a grandma-aged woman and neighborhood children do together.

> TEACHER: As I read this story to you, I want each group to focus on one part of the story. I would like everyone in group A to draw a picture of what Miss Tizzy and the children do on Monday. Everyone in Group B will focus on Tuesday and draw a picture, Group C will draw what happens on Wednesday, Group D will draw Thursday's event, and Group E will draw Friday's activities. (*Halfway through the story, the teacher stops reading and gives the groups time to draw their pictures. When all the pictures had been drawn, the teacher continues.*) As I read the rest of the story, I want each group to focus on the same day as before, but this time I want everyone to draw a picture of what the children do for Miss Tizzy. All of you in Group A will draw the first activity, each student in Group B will draw the next activity, and so on.

After the teacher finished the story, the groups drew their pictures. After the students had completed their pictures, the students gathered as a class. With input from the students, the teacher placed the pictures on the whiteboard in order of when they occurred in the story.

TEACHER: We learned what Miss Tizzy and the children did that was special for each day of the week. Let's think of what our class does that is special on each day of the week. Keep with the same day that you focused on in the story. Discuss with your group what happens in our class on that day, and everyone in your group can draw a picture. (*Later.*) Today, when you get home from school, talk to your parents about special things that you do each day outside of school. On the chart I have given you (see figure 5.5), draw a picture or place stickers to show something that you do each day of the school week. On my chart, for example, I put a sticker of a grandmother, because I visit my grandmother every Monday. Every Tuesday, I watched my son play soccer. (*Pauses.*) We often organize our time around days of the week. Why do you think we use days of the week to organize us?

MARALEE: We might need some special supplies each day. If I think of soccer on Tuesday, then I can be sure that all of my clothes and equipment are ready that day.

STEPHEN: If I know that there is a spelling test every Friday, then I can study ahead of time.

TEACHER: How do calendars help your parents?

BOBBY: They know when to go to soccer practice, doctor's appointments, buy birthdays gifts, prepare for holidays.

	Monday	Tuesday	Wednesday	Thursday	Friday
Miss Tizzy and the Children	Baked cookies	Made up stories, puppet shows	Played parade music	Drew pictures	Played dress-up
The Children	Brought cookies to Miss Tizzy	Puppet show outside Miss Tizzy's window	Played a soft drumming sound	Drew pictures and left them in Miss Tizzy's mailbox	Put on funny hats, and left a tea tray for Miss Tizzy
Our Class	Library	Art	Music	Computer lab	A Play
Me	Grandma	Soccer			

Figure 5.5 The Sequencing Chart helps students organize information.

TEACHER: We can organize events in a different way. You could draw a happy face chart (see figure 5.6), and place five things you do in order of your most favorite to your least favorite. In my chart, I would put playing with my puppy under the four happy faces and cleaning my house in the column with no happy faces. What are some things you put under four happy faces?

AMANDA: Riding my bike.

JORDAN: I put cooking with my grandma.

TEACHER: When do we organize ideas or things based on how much we like them?

TESSA: When we want to decide what we like to do with our free time.

LAURA: When we need to decide how to spend our money.

DAVID: It can help me to decide how to spend time with my family and friends.

TEACHER: We have learned that we can sequence or order things for days of the week, or events during the year, or based on how important things are to us.

☺☺☺☺	☺☺☺	☺☺	☺	

Figure 5.6 For younger students, a happy-face chart can be used for sequencing.

SCHEMA-GENERAL QUESTIONS

Rationale

Many sets of questions in instructional materials appear to interfere with, rather than enhance, comprehension. The questions suggested in teachers' manuals, for instance, are not likely to help students organize and internalize key ideas of a topic. Therefore, students need to know how to ask their own questions based on the logical organization of events and ideas of central importance to the story. Students also need to be taught how to connect events and ideas and be introduced to story grammars.

Description

Singer and Donlon (1982) developed a strategy called Schema-General Questions to connect the relationships in narrative (story) structure. With this strategy, students decide upon the starting point of the story and then list in summary form the major events and ideas that make up the plot and the links between events, or the gist of the story. Implied ideas that are part of the story but are not directly stated are included. Finally, students ask questions to glean information that matches the progression of ideas and events.

Specifically, students are taught to ask themselves questions about the following, in oral or written format: (1) main character, (2) goal, (3) problem, (4) resolution, and (5) theme.

Main Character

- Who is the main character?
- What does the character do?
- What have I learned about the character from what he or she has done?

Goal

- What does the main character want?
- What have I learned about the main character after discovering his or her goal?
- What does the main character do to reach his or her goal?
- What have I learned about the main character from what that character has done?

Problem

- What is the first problem that the main character has?
- What does the main character do about it?
- How does the main character change as a result of the problem?
- What does this tell me about the main character?

Resolution

- Does the main character get what he or she wants?
- What has most helped the character: forces within that character's control or forces beyond that character's control? Name them.

Theme

- Does the story basically tell about (1) a struggle with self, (2) a struggle with nature, (3) a struggle with others?

Example

Using this strategy, a third-grade class logically organized the events and ideas in Brian Birchall's book, *Kahu, the Cautious Kiwi*. Figure 5.7 is one student's written summary of the story, using Singer and Donlon's format:

SCHEMA-GENERAL QUESTIONS

Name: _____Juline_____ Date: _____November 23_____

Book Title: _____Kahu, the Cautious Kiwi_____

Using the questions you have learned to ask yourself,
write a summary of the book under the following headings:

The Main Character: Kahu, the kiwi, is the main character. A kiwi is a very shy kind of bird that lives in New Zealand. Kahu is too big to live with his parents anymore, so he goes off to live by himself in a rimu tree. I learned about Kahu that he was very brave to go out on his own and his growing up.

The Goal: Kahu just wants to live a peaceful life sleeping all day and looking for worms and grubs all night. I learned that kiwis have very simple lives. He doesn't really want much except to be left alone. It's not really a goal, but that's what he tries to do just by going about his life.

The Problem: A pig hunter and his dogs come along, and the dogs chased Kahu. He ran into the bush to get away, and his foot got caught in a trap. A wild cat tried to attack Kahu, but Kahu hit the cat's face with his other claw. Kahu is changed because he's frightened and all alone. I bet he wishes he hadn't left his family.

The Resolution: Kahu got the peaceful life he wanted but not right away. First a boy comes along and gets Kahu out of the trap. He takes Kahu home with him, and they become friends. He helps his leg get well. He follows the boy around. He follows him to school, and the teacher sees him. The teacher says kiwis are protected birds and the boy should take him back to the bush. So forces beyond Kahu's control got Kahu what he wanted, because the boy let him go in the bush and he was really happy.

The Theme: This story told mostly about a struggle of a kiwi against the world, because he would have been happy in nature, but manufactured things like traps caused him to have big problems.

See BLM 9 in appendix for reproducible master.

Figure 5.7 A young student used the Schema-General Questions strategy to summarize the story *Kahu, the Cautious Kiwi*.

VISUAL (DIGITAL) LITERACY

Rationale

An old saying imparts this wisdom: "A picture speak a thousand words." Many students need visual stimulation to help them understand the world around them – that is, to help them internalize what they are reading. Today's students are growing up in a digital world. They can analyze stories and then create their own parallel stories using digital cameras and story-making software. With this strategy, students learn to look at different points of view, create a plan with a sequence, and apply the concept to their own lives and experiences.

Description

Students can use digital photos that are online, or use digital cameras to take their own pictures. They can draw their own pictures and scan them to use on the computer or find free clip art online (or available with a software program). Specific sites can be bookmarked to insure safe searching. You can have students design a project as a whole class and then divide the class into small groups, with each group responsible for part of the project. Alternately, small groups can work together to create several different stories (theme and variation). After students have had several class experiences using the Visual Literacy strategy, each student can work on his or her own project.

Projects may focus on storytelling, with a beginning, middle, and end. Students can create characters, settings, problems, and plot developments. You may want projects to have a particular focus, such as social studies or science.

Example

Rosie's Walk is a book written for young children by Pat Hutchins. Rosie is a chicken who goes for a walk throughout the barnyard.

TEACHER: Who can tell us what happened to Rosie in the story?

BEN: The fox followed Rosie the chicken, but she did not know the fox was there.

CATHY: She went over the fence, around the haystack, and all around the farmyard. The fox kept tripping and running into trouble.

LYNN: Rosie went back to the barn safely without the fox hurting her.

TEACHER: Yes, the fox followed Rosie but made many mistakes, which kept Rosie safe. Rosie went under, around, and through different things on the farm....I have an idea – let's plan a trip around our playground, the school, or the neighborhood. I will divide you into small groups of three. In your groups, you will plan part of a walk. Just as Rosie did, you will walk under, around, through, or over something.

After grouping the students, the teacher took the students on a short field trip so that they could plan their part of the walk.

TEACHER: When we get back into the classroom, I want all groups to give me one of their plans, and I will write each plan on the whiteboard. If two groups give me the same plan, the second group will need to give me a different plan. (*Back in the classroom after the short field trip, each group shares one part of its walk.*) Two of the groups plan to walk under the tree. Can you think of something else that we can walk under?

CLAUDIA: In our group, we want to walk under the monkey bars.

TEACHER: Okay. Now, using information from the whiteboard, I want you, in your groups, to draw a map of your walk. You can draw pictures or use symbols to help you remember your route. You are also going to take photographs of the places you drew a picture or symbol. Each group may have a different story. Is everyone ready to go back outside? Choose one person in your group to take the pictures, and I will give that person a camera. (*Pauses.*) I have asked our sixth-grade buddies to come with us and help you. When we are back in the classroom, your buddies will help you download the pictures onto the computer, choose the photographs you want to keep, and arrange the pictures for your groups.

Later, back in the classroom, buddies helped the students download their pictures onto the computer. Students then used the computer as a learner center, with groups taking turns importing their pictures into a software program (e.g., *Kidpix*). Next, students posted their pictures on their class website, making their work available for their parents and grandparents to see.

Related Information

This strategy can also be used with older students, as in the following example. Students worked on a digital project that involved the five geographic themes: (1) location, (2) place, (3) human-environment interaction, (4) region, and (5) movement. After brainstorming examples and discussing these themes, students used digital cameras to take pictures in their neighborhood of the five themes, imported the pictures into presentation software, and then added slides to explain their choices. The students then began work on a history project about different cultures. They read *Talking Walls* by Margy Burns Knight and illustrator Anne Sibley O'Brien. The book (and software) shows walls that tell stories of different cultures, locations, and histories from all over the world. By understanding the walls – that may surround, protect, or divide – the students began to understand a bit about the people who lived by the walls.

TEACHER: Do you suppose other communities in other parts of the United States – or even other parts of the world – have walls that tell about the people who live nearby?

ANDY: I visited my cousin in Vermont. They have a tile wall at their playground. Each student designed a tile. My cousin drew his family on his tile.

TEACHER: We could use ePals to ask your cousin to send us a picture. What could we ask other students in other countries?

BRYAN: We could ask them to take a picture or draw a picture and send it to us.

Students may communicate with other communities (for example, www.ePals.com) to share what they know about their own community and to ask students in other parts of the world to explore and share about their cultures and communities.

CHAPTER 6
Student Questioning Strategies for Intermediate Grades

The cruxes of critical thinking are reflection and the ability to consider a host of possible alternatives. As students move into the intermediate grades, they are ready to experience a greater degree of independence in their thinking. This is the time to encourage them to ask their own thoughtful questions about content as they begin to make sense of what they read in fresh and original ways.

DYAD READING

Rationale

Paired oral reading experiences have two advantages: (1) large numbers of students can practice reading at the same time; and (2) both students in each pair are actively involved at all times, either as reader or listener. With Dyad Reading, or two-person reading, a third advantage is added: one student must purposefully listen to the other, then summarize what was just said. The reader then asks the listener a critical question from the text. Students quickly learn to ask each other higher-level questions rather than those that require simple yes or no answers.

Description

Dyad Reading is a form of reciprocal oral reading that has the added dimension of increasing important critical-thinking skills through summarizing and questioning. You can teach the strategy using the following format:

1. Select two students, and have one read a paragraph aloud. (With younger children, one paragraph can be reduced to one sentence.)

2. As that student reads, have the other student listen and then summarize (aloud or in writing) what was in the paragraph. (For variation, the second student may draw what was read, then describe the picture.)

3. Have the reader ask the listener critical-thinking questions.

4. Encourage the students to discuss the answers and, where there is disagreement, have them refer back to the paragraph to support their answers.

5. Have the students reverse roles.

When you feel the students are ready to practice this strategy independently, divide the class into pairs or threesomes. (In a threesome, a child who is a limited-English speaker or a nonreader can get the gist of the passage by listening to it being read first, then hearing it being summarized.)

Example

Three fifth-grade students were reading Nina Bawden's *The Outside Child*. The book is about a young girl who finds out she has a half brother and a half sister.

Lila read the following paragraph aloud:

> It was easier talking to Plato's mother than I would have expected. She had asked a question occasionally, but until she thought of Pandora she had listened in silence, sitting on the end of the couch. She had made me lie down on it to "rest" as if I were an invalid. Plato was sitting on the floor, back against the wall, hugging his knees and listening with a broody expression. I had told them what had actually happened. What I hadn't told them was how I had felt when Amy had started to scream. That once ages ago I must have done something dreadfully wicked. It seemed too shameful to mention (Bawden 1994, 141).

SAMANTHA (*Summarizing the paragraph.*): Jane was worried about talking to Plato's mother, but it's no big deal. She turns out to be a pretty good listener. She feels really ashamed of what she is telling them, and she's wondering what Plato's reaction will be.

The third child, Rachel, spoke little English but was able to quickly sketch her understanding of the paragraph, augmented by Samantha's summary. She shared her picture with Lila and Samantha.

TEACHER: Lila, can you add anything to the summary?

LILA: Jane also was lying down because Plato's mother kept treating her like an invalid. (*To Samantha.*) What do you think Jane was expecting Plato's mother to do when she heard her story? If it was easier than she thought, what do you think she expected to have happened?

SAMANTHA: I think she expected Plato's mother to be shocked.

LILA: Why would she have been shocked? She told them what happened, but not everything. The bad parts she left out. See...it says, "What I hadn't told them was how I felt when Amy had started to scream....It seemed too shameful to mention."

WONDERING NOTEBOOKS

Rationale

Students are often enthusiastic questioners by the time they enter elementary school. Most parents have experienced endless "why" conversations with their children (when children ask a question, followed by "why" after the parent answers, followed by another why). At some point, most children stop asking why. The Wondering Notebooks strategy encourages them to start asking why questions again and enter into "a school of curiosity." Jones and Leahy (2006) relate this model to reading comprehension, but it can have a broader application.

Description

Wondering questions are very broad and have a philosophical bent to them. They often encompass more than one discipline, thus, students may use a variety of perspectives. Harvey and Goudvis (2000) recommend the following steps:

1. Model some specific examples of wondering questions for your students.
2. Give each student a Wondering Notebook. Have students record in the notebook any questions that they have been thinking about.
3. After seeing a video, listening to an assembly, or studying science, ask students if they have any questions. For instance, after studying electricity, students might wonder how a remote control or a garage-door opener works.
4. After reading a story or a book, students might think of questions they would ask the author if they met him or her.
5. Have students share their questions with the class.
6. Categorize the questions. Reread the questions in each category to see if there is a "mega question" or an "over-arching" question.

To enable students to address the questions, design lessons, assign research projects, or set up learning centers.

Example

The teacher wanted to introduce the Wondering Notebooks strategy to her students.

TEACHER: Today we are going to learn about wondering questions. I'm going to begin by giving you some examples of my wondering questions:

*   Why does the snow melt under trees first (where it is shady) and not where it is sunny just beyond the trees?
*   Why do we have customs?
*   Does everyone in the world laugh when they are happy? Does everyone cry when they are sad?
*   Why can airplanes fly and I can't? (Airplanes are much heavier than I am.)
*   Why do some pictures look like I can walk into them? How does the artist do that?

- How do astronauts go to the bathroom?
- Sometimes on windy days it feels as though the wind could whisk me away. Could it?

I am now going to give each of you a notebook so you can write down your wondering questions. You can add wondering questions to your notebook all year long.

After giving students time to write down and discuss some wondering questions of their own, the teacher had students read the book *Bridge to Terabitha* by Katherine Paterson.

TEACHER: Now that you have read the book, do you have some wondering questions about the book?

The students had several questions about the characters:

- What will it be like when Jess and Maybelle are 10 years older?
- Why did the author write such a sad story?
- What happened to Jess after the story ended?
- What did Jess do when he was older? Was he a runner? Was he an artist?
- Why did the author have a boy and a girl become friends. Is it not unusual for boys and girls to be friends in fifth grade?
- Did the author know some children like Jess and Leslie?

TEACHER: Can we group some of these questions together?

RALPH: There were a couple of questions about the future, after the story ended.

EDIE: There were some questions for the author.

TEACHER: Do you think we might be able to find some answers to these questions, or find some information that might lead to a good guess?

TOM: Some authors have websites, and sometimes other people have written about authors. We could check the Internet.

TEACHER: Any other ideas?

PAULA: Maybe we could email the author or call her and see if she will answer our questions.

The students then separated their questions about characters into two categories: (1) while the story was taking place, and (2) after the story ended.

The students researched online and found answers to some but not to all of the questions. They decided to send their unanswered questions to the author. They also asked the author if she might visit their school or talk to them on the phone or over the Internet.

I-SEARCH

Rationale

Searching for information about a topic of special interest and then connecting the ideas from that search to others is an adventure in learning. The I-Search strategy helps children search for critical information and realize that there is a personal story behind every research paper (even though the pronoun *I* is rarely used in such writing). The strategy helps students develop research skills while offering them the experience of telling the background story about the search for information.

Description

Freedman (1986) suggests teaching students to use I-Search in three phases: (1) problem identification, (2) information quest, and (3) writing the paper.

Problem Identification

With the students, brainstorm a list of topics in which they are interested. When they have chosen their favorite from among these topics, have them, as a group, write statements about the topic, followed by a list of questions they have about the topic.

Information Quest

Model for students how they can use the Internet, library references, and trade books, or interview resource people to get the information they need to answer their questions.

Writing the Paper

Give students a specific format to follow – one that requires that they ask themselves three key questions about the research task. They will ask two of the questions before they begin research and one question when the research has been completed:

1. What do I want to know? [statement of the problem]
2. How will I find the information I need? [procedures]
3. What did I find out? [summary]

After introducing this activity to the class, implement it with individual students or in small cooperative groups. Write topic suggestions on the whiteboard, and put any information the students already have about the topic in a separate column. Next, provide each student or group with an I-Search activity sheet (see figure 6.1).

By asking their own questions, students are introduced to the fundamentals of research (including the preparation of bibliographies). With the I-Search sheet providing the essential format for a research paper, the writer's task is then to flesh out the sections and combine them into a complete report. An I-Search activity sheet reminds students of the procedures they must follow and of the critical questions they must ask themselves.

Example

Two students, working as partners, used the I-Search strategy to learn about Hispanics.

1. What do I want to know? The children, both Hispanic, brainstormed, decided on a topic to investigate, then formed the question, How have Hispanics contributed to American life? They wrote the question at the top of their activity sheet. They discussed, then wrote down in the information section, all the things they could think of that they already knew about their topic and any questions they had.

I-SEARCH		
Name: _Juan and Michael_ Date: _February 16_		
Question: _How have Hispanics contributed to American life?_		
What do I/we already know?	**Information:** Hispanics contribute to American life in many ways. We celebrate Cinco de Mayo because of them and they speak Spanish. We have lots of Mexican restaurants.	
How do I/we find the information I/we need?	**Source:** Franco, John. Hispano American Contributors to American Life. Benefic Press, 1990.	**What the Sources Said:** There have been educators, scientists, businessmen, actors, entertainers, athletes, physicians, government officials, and labor leaders who were famous.
	Current Biography Yearbook. H.W. Wilson Company, 2009.	Many Hispanics were prejudiced against and grew up poor. It was hard for them to succeed, but some worked hard and made it.
What did I/we discover?	1. Hispanics are important in every part of American society. 2. Some Hispanics are very poor and have a hard life. They experience lots of prejudice. Not everyone appreciates what they have to offer. 3. Hispanics have contributed to every part of our lives: they have been doctors, lawyers, scientists, government officials, entertainers, actors, and athletes.	

Figure 6.1 Students used the I-Search Activity Sheet as they researched Hispanics.

See BLM 10 in appendix for reproducible master.

2. How do I find the information I need? With teacher guidance, the students found two resources: *Hispanic American Contributors to American Life*, a trade book, and a reference book, *Current Biography Yearbook*. They wrote down the bibliographic information as well as the information that they got from these sources.

3. What did I find out? The students summarized the results of their investigation, and, where necessary, revised statements they had made prior to doing the research. In this case, they had a startling – and welcome – revelation when they discovered their heritage was a good deal more rich than just tacos and *cinco de mayo*, as they had previously thought.

QUESTION GENERATING

Rationale

Question Generating (Cooper 1993) is a strategy used to help students improve their ability to construct meaning. Students generate their own questions about the text, then find the answers through reading.

Carefully modeled by competent teachers, Question Generating may be the most useful strategy of all for promoting the construction of meaning before, during, and after reading. The strategy could have little value, however, if it is not well taught (Pressley et al. 1990).

Description

The process involves showing children how to ask key questions so that they assimilate important information as they read. To do this, students need to learn to internalize the following steps as they read:

1. Skim the material to be read.
   - Look at the cover and illustrations.
   - Read titles and subtitles.
   - Read the introduction and summary.
2. Ask a question about the topic.
   - Make the title into a question.
   - Write it down.
3. Read the passage to find answers to the question.
   - Write down the answer.
   - Decide if the question is a good critical question.
   - Revise the question, if necessary.
4. Ask another question about the topic.
   - Decide if this question can be answered from the reading.
   - Write down the question.

5. Read more of the passage to find answers to the question, and continue to think of questions while reading.
   - Write down questions.
   - Write down answers.
6. Save questions that cannot be answered through the passage for research to do at a later time.

Example

A fourth-grade student used the Question Generating strategy to construct meaning of the text, "Young Man with a Mission: Albert Schweitzer," edited by R. L. Whitehead.

1. Skim the material. The student skimmed the text, looking at the illustrations and reading the first paragraph (some expository text has no introduction or summary).

2. Ask a question about the topic. The student wrote down the question, What was Albert Schweitzer's mission?

3. Read the passage to answer your question. The student read the passage and wrote the following answer to her question, Albert Schweitzer's mission, was to become a medical missionary in Africa and to help the people there. She then considered whether or not she had asked a good critical question. She decided it was, as most of the passage concerned Schweitzer's medical mission in Africa.

4. Ask another question about the topic. The student thought about what she had read so far, then wrote, Did Schweitzer ever regret his decision to become a medical missionary?

5. Read more of the passage to find the answers to your question. The student read on, and her question was soon answered. She wrote,

   Albert Schweitzer had made up his mind and nothing could change it. He did not have enough money to go to the university, and they tried to persuade him to give up his dream. His wife got sick and had to go and live in Switzerland, and he could only see her once in a while. But still he loved what he was doing and was very successful at healing lots of people. No, I don't think he ever regretted it.

6. Save questions that cannot be answered through the passage for research to do at a later time. The student, fascinated by Albert Schweitzer, wrote down the following questions:
   - Is Dr. Schweitzer's hospital still running in Lambarene?
   - How did he die?
   - Did the people in Africa ever wonder why a white man would help them that way?
   - Did he ever get any bad diseases?
   - Did he ever win any awards for his courage?

COGNITIVE STRATEGY INSTRUCTION IN WRITING

Rationale

A strategy that has proven effective in helping students do expository writing is the Cognitive Strategy Instruction in Writing (CSIW) (Raphael and Englebert 1990). Incorporating a writing strategy with reading can improve students' ability to do expository writing, help them understand different organizational structures, and improve their ability to construct their own meaning through self-questioning (Konapale, Martin, and Martin 1990).

Description

CSIW has been used with intermediate-grade students to help them write and read expository material, by having them ask their own questions. The strategy is based upon four principles: (1) text analysis, (2) modeling, (3) guided practice, and (4) independent writing.

Text Analysis

Model for the students how to analyze a piece of writing in terms of the text structure – sequence, problem/solution, enumeration, comparison, description, or cause/effect. For the demonstration, use something you have written, or select a passage from a book.

Modeling

Select a topic that fits with a specific organizational structure for writing, then use a Think Sheet to model how you plan and organize a piece of writing (see figure 6.2). The following questions are useful:

- What is my topic?
- Who am I writing for?
- What do I already know about the topic?
- Where can I get more information?
- What organizational structure makes sense?
- What are some beginning ideas?
- What are some ending ideas?

Guided Practice

Have the students select their own topics and write their own papers, soliciting guidance from you as necessary.

Independent Writing

After plenty of guided practice, using several different organizational structures, give each student a Think Sheet. Have students plan and organize their own writing independently. Encourage them to combine several structures, as writers often do.

Example

A fourth-grade student used the CSIW strategy to write an expository piece about bathing his dog (see figure 6.2). (This was his first attempt at using CSIW on his own.)

CSIW

Name: _Randy H._ Date: _January 18_

Topic: _Bathing a dog_

What is my topic?

Giving your dog a bath

Who am I writing for?

My family, teacher, and classmates will read this.

What do I already know about this topic?

I give my dog a bath every week and I'm really good at it but most people aren't. Most dogs hate to take a bath.

Where can I get more information about this topic?

The Internet has lots of information. There is also a magazine called Pet Care that you can find in the library. I also read other books about dogs and pets.

What organizational structure should I use?

You have to do everything in the right order, so I think I should use Sequence.

What are some beginning ideas?

Lots of dogs like mine don't like to get baths so you have to bribe them. I will talk about how I bribe Laddie with a toy mouse or a dog bone.

What are some ending ideas?

How my dog looks as good as new after a bath and you feel proud and the dog does too.

See BLM 11 in appendix for reproducible master.

Figure 6.2 CSIW is a useful strategy for writing expository pieces.

METACOGNITIVE READING

Rationale

When students read in school, they need to be guided in developing metacognitive (or self-monitoring) reading strategies so that these important skills become an internalized part of their normal reading behavior. This Metacognitive Reading strategy gives readers a sense of how much or how little they are bringing to the reading task, what the task is, and what is expected of them. The strategy helps readers know when and if their comprehension is failing them and what they should do to correct the situation.

Description

The School District of Philadelphia developed a Metacognitive Reading strategy through the MERIT Chapter 2 Project (1986) that significantly helped students monitor their own comprehension. The proponents explain that when a reader is reading fluently with adequate comprehension, he or she is said to be "c-l-i-c-k-i-n-g a-l-o-n-g." But when something comes along that is not understood – an unfamiliar word, reference, or idea, for example – the reader hits a "c-l-u-n-k." A proficient reader usually realizes that a problem has been encountered and takes steps to correct it. This strategy delineates the seven steps needed to correct a problem in comprehension, adapted here to a self-questioning format.

1. Am I reading too fast? Students need to be taught that a social studies textbook, for example, should not be read at the same speed as a mystery story. Students need, therefore, to first question the rate at which they are trying to read the material to determine if they should be reading at a more careful rate.

2. Will the author explain the "clunk" if I continue reading? Often a word, idea, or reference will be explained satisfactorily if the reader is patient and waits for the meaning to be cleared up through the context or by the addition of new information.

3. Should I reread what I just read? Often a passage makes more sense to the reader a second time; sometimes, a word that has been decoded incorrectly or omitted is corrected upon rereading.

4. Should I study the diagrams, maps, charts, graphs, or other aids the text has provided? Much information is provided in diagrams in expository material, and students need to learn to study these important additions to texts.

5. Can I look up an unfamiliar word or term in the glossary, the dictionary, or my textbook? When vocabulary is the issue, students need to accept their lack of knowledge and know what they can do to rectify it.

6. Should I talk to another classmate about this problem or question? In a child-centered classroom, students feel free to try to straighten out the comprehension barrier through discussion with a trusted friend. Often talking through a comprehension problem helps the student work it out.

7. Could the teacher help with this problem? Because the essence of positive metacognitive self-questioning skills is to help the student become an independent thinker, this final step is a last resort. But if the student is aware that he or she is not comprehending, this is a good strategy. After exhausting all other resources, you or another adult can often shed some light on what the possible problem might be.

Example

A sixth-grade boy was reading a passage titled "Catalonia, a Modern Country with Centuries of Tradition." The transcript of the boy's questions and answers to himself shows how the child used Metacognitive Reading strategy to work out a comprehension problem.

The student read:

> Catalonia, a country in Spain with its own culture, language, and identity, has its Patron Saint's day, Saint Jordi, on April 23. And on this day the rose and the book become part of Catalonia itself.

The boy was confused. He did not understand how a rose and a book were "part of Catalonia." What did that mean?

He began to go through his hierarchy of questions in the Metacognitive Reading strategy.

1. Am I reading too fast? Maybe I am. This is about social studies, and I know I am supposed to slow down for work-type reading. I'll slow down a little, but I don't think that's the problem.

2. Will the author explain the "clunk" if I continue reading? Okay, I'll try that and see.

   He read the next sentence:

   > The rose represents coexistence, affection, and community spirit, and the book stands for culture and love of language.

   Oh, I get it, the boy thought. The book and the rose are like symbols for things. The people of the country use them to mean what they feel about their country. But now I am confused by the word *coexistence*. I don't know what that means.

3. Should I reread what I just read? I reread it, and I still don't understand that word, but I'm quite sure that I was right about the rose and book being symbols for other things. I'm just not sure of what the rose is a symbol for.

4. Should I study the diagrams, maps, charts, graphs, or other aids the text has provided? There is a map here, and it shows me that Catalonia is a little part of Spain and that Barcelona is a city that is in it. That helps, but it doesn't tell me everything about this word, I don't think.

5. Can I look up an unfamiliar word or term in the glossary, the dictionary, or in my textbook? This book doesn't have a glossary, and I can't find an answer in my textbook. I'll look it up in my dictionary. It says that coexistence means "existing together or at the same time." I still don't understand what it means that the rose represents existing together.

6. Should I talk to a classmate about this problem or question? I'll try that. [He read the passage aloud to his friend Tony, and asked him what he thought it meant.] Tony said he thinks it's talking about the people of Catalonia existing together in peace, kind of like English people and French people in Canada live together, or coexist. I think Tony is right – that makes sense to me.

7. Should I talk to the teacher? At this point, the student had no need to consult the teacher, and he was able to complete the passage successfully, continuing to ask himself questions about his construction of meaning of the passage.

SURVEY, QUESTION, READ, RECITE, AND REVIEW

Rationale

Study methods are strategies that students can learn in order to help them study written material in ways that enhance comprehension through self-questioning and answering. Such strategies are student-directed, rather than teacher-directed, and are implemented to help students remember content material better than they would remember it by simply reading the material. Probably the best-known of these strategies is Robinson's (1961) Survey, Question, Read, Recite, and Review (SQ3R).

Description

It is important that you take the time in class to show students how to go through the various steps of SQ3R and hold group practice sessions before the students perform the steps independently. In time, the steps will begin to become ingrained in the students' minds.

1. Survey. Select a passage, then, with the students, survey the selection, reading aloud the chapter titles and main headings, introductory and summary paragraphs, and inspecting and discussing any visual aids, such as maps, graphs, or illustrations. Explain that this initial survey provides a framework for organizing the facts that will later be derived from the reading.

2. Question. Show the students how to formulate questions from chapter headings, main headings, and titles. These questions, which provide a good purpose for reading, should be answered in the next section. Encourage students to generate other questions, and add ones that you expect the students might be able to answer from the reading.

3. Read. With the students, read the selection to find answers to the questions that have been formulated. You may want to make brief notes on the whiteboard to model behavior that students can follow. (This is purposeful reading, and making brief notes may be helpful.)

4. Recite. Have the students try to answer each of the questions formulated earlier, without looking at the passage.

5. Review. With the students, reread the passage to verify or correct your recited answers, to make sure you have the main points of the selection in mind, and to help you understand the relationships among the various points.

Example

A fourth-grade class was preparing to read a chapter in social studies titled, "The Westward Movement." Guided by their teacher, they went through the steps in SQ3R.

Survey

The students looked over the chapter briefly and then read the title, the main heading, the introduction, and the summary together.

Question

The students turned the chapter title, "The Westward Movement," into the question, What was the westward movement? The teacher listed other questions from headings and subheadings on the whiteboard.

- When did the westward movement happen?
- Why did it take place?
- Who was involved?
- Where did they go?
- What was it like to go westward?

Read

The students read the selection to find answers to their questions.

Recite

Without looking at the chapter, the students answered the questions aloud. Because they had asked their own questions, they found the answers easier to remember.

Review

There was a difference of opinion in response to the question, Why did the westward movement take place? One boy believed it was to search for a better life; another was certain it was to find gold. The students went back to the text to settle the disagreement. (They were both correct.) Each boy supported his answer by reading the information from the text.

Related Information

Newspapers provide excellent vehicles through which to practice this kind of questioning, but the steps followed vary slightly from that in SQ3R. After choosing an article of interest, have the child follow these six steps (Cecil 1994):

1. Skim the article quickly.
2. List four questions you have about the article.
3. Read the article to find answers to your questions.
4. Rewrite the article, answering the questions.
5. Recite from memory all you have learned from the article.
6. List any questions you still have about the subject.

CHAPTER 7
Questions Across
the Curriculum

In far too many classrooms, subjects such as language arts and science are isolated into separate disciplines that promote neither depth of understanding nor connections with other subjects. Learning is assumed to take place primarily through one vehicle – the textbook – and this is frequently not read by the students (Armbruster 1991; Howes, Limm, and Campos 2008; Kinniburgh and Shaw 2009). Rather, the textbook is read aloud by the teacher, or the information from it is simply told to the students. By contrast, learning across the curriculum is interactive, inviting all students to access knowledge through a variety of problem-solving experiences that can best be tied together through effective questioning strategies.

All the ideas and principles presented in this book apply as we now begin to think about questioning across the curricular areas of math, science, social studies, and art appreciation. Examples of questioning strategies introduced in chapters 3–6, as well as new ones, are presented as they are applied and connected in a variety of content areas.

QUESTIONING IN MATHEMATICS

Questioning can help teachers connect mathematics to the rest of the curricular areas, for the goals of mathematics are remarkably similar to those of other disciplines, both cognitively and affectively. Through these goals, learners develop the following (Hyde and Bizar 1989; Franke et al. 2009):

- Knowledge of math and concepts in related areas
- Ability to problem solve, think critically, and monitor one's own thinking
- Confidence and positive attitudes about self

Let us now see how several teachers in different classrooms used questioning techniques to achieve these goals.

Vignette 1, Grade 4
Integration: Math/Oral Language

TEACHER: I'm going to ask you a question for which we won't be able to get an exact answer, but I want to find out if we can come close. How many golf balls do you think will fit inside this suitcase? (*Allows the students to examine the suitcase and a golf ball.*)

RANDY: Do you want us to just guess? I guess there would be room for 300!

TEACHER: Thanks for your response, Randy. You may be right, but does anyone have any idea how we could be more sure of our answer? (*Pauses, then calls on Jessica.*)

JESSICA: Could we fill up the suitcase with golf balls and find out? Then we would know for sure, I think.

TEACHER: That is one sure way, Jessica, but we have only one golf ball. Any other ideas? (*Pauses.*) José?

JOSÉ: How about if we measure the golf ball and the suitcase?

JESSICA: Yes, let's do that! (*The teacher selects three students to measure the golf ball and three to measure the suitcase.*)

JOSÉ (*On behalf of the suitcase group.*): The suitcase is 24 inches wide and 30 inches long and 8 inches high.[1]

RANDY (*On behalf of the golf ball group.*): If the ball was square, it would be about one inch by one inch.

TEACHER: So – can anyone tell me approximately how many golf balls will fit in that suitcase? (*Pauses, then, realizing the students may have forgotten how to solve the problem of finding cubic inches, prompts.*) If the suitcase is 30 inches by 24 inches by 8 inches, can anyone estimate what the answer to this would be by multiplying the three numbers together? (*Jessica begins to compute, using paper and pencil.*) Remember – we are not looking for an exact answer, just an approximation. (*Prompts.*) What numbers might you use to estimate if you wanted to do the problem in your head?

JESSICA: Thirty by twenty by ten? Is that right, to round 'em off? (*The teacher smiles and nods.*) About 6000 golf balls. Wow – 6000 golf balls, more or less, would fit in that suitcase.

RANDY: I was way off. The way we thought about it was way better than guessing!

---

1. The metric size of the suitcase is 70 cm wide, 77 cm high, and 20 cm high. The golf ball is about 2.5 cm by 2.5 cm.

Vignette 2, Grade 5
Integration: Math/Oral Language/Listening

In this classroom, the teacher used Think Aloud to provide "beginning thinkers" with a way to observe "expert thinking," usually hidden from their view.

TEACHER: We might have to use this type of problem when we have only parts of a whole. For instance, suppose I have two pizzas. One pizza is cut into six equal pieces, and four pieces are left. The other pizza was cut into three equal pieces, and two pieces are left. Will I have enough pizza to serve seven friends and me an equal size of pizza? What do I do when I face a problem like this: 4/6 + 2/3? I know how to add fractions when the denominator is the same, such as 5/6 + 1/6, but I have no general procedure for adding them when the denominators are different, as in this problem. For the time being, probably the best I can do is look at some simple examples for a clue about how this is done. Okay, here's an example: 3/4 + 1/8. What they do is make both of the denominators the same by going 3/4 = 6/8. When I look at this for a while, I realize that 8 is twice as much as 4 (*Pauses to let all learners follow her thinking.*), and, hey, 6 is twice as much as 3. I think I will try that with my problem. Does someone want to help me with my hunch? (*Pauses.*) Nuri?

NURI: You can make both fractions the same by making 2/3 into a fraction with 6 at the bottom. You say 2/3 = ?/6, and then you say 6 is twice as much as 3, so what is twice as much as 2? The answer is 4! So 2/3 = 4/6.

TEACHER: Good thinking, Nuri! Now the problem is just like the ones I already know how to do, such as adding fractions when they're the same: 4/6 + 4/6 = 8/6. Does anyone want to add their thoughts to mine?

Vignette 3, Grade K
Integration: Math/Oral Language

The teacher in this primary classroom provided an integration of linguistic, conceptual, and mathematical experiences for her young learners as she structured their play with attribute blocks of varying colors, sizes, and shapes.

TEACHER (*To students who are seated in small groups, with one bag of blocks per group.*): Can anyone think of a way we could group these blocks? (*Pauses.*) Cary, Chelsea, and Ben?

CARY: I pulled out all the red pieces. See?

TEACHER: All the red pieces. That is a way to group the blocks. Chelsea?

CHELSEA: I got all the blue pieces.

TEACHER: Yes, Chelsea, you sorted them in the same way Cary did – by color. Can you think of another way to group them, Chelsea?

CHELSEA: Ummm, now I got all the circles together. (*The teacher nods and looks at Ben.*)

BEN: These blocks are all big, and these ones are all little.

TEACHER: Yes, Ben. Does everyone see that Ben has grouped his blocks according to their size? That is another way to group the blocks. Anything else? Can anyone use two ways to group the blocks? (*Prompts.*) For example, can anyone use size and color? Ben and Chelsea?

BEN: See, these are little and blue!

TEACHER: Yes, very good! They are all alike in two ways: They have the same size and the same color. Chelsea?

CHELSEA: Mine are all green, and they are all small.

TEACHER: Chelsea also grouped the blocks by size and color, but a different size and a different color from Ben's.

Vignette 4, Grade 1
Integration: Math/Oral Language

The teacher wanted students to understand that clear communication and problem solving involve defining terms and seeing situations from more than one point of view.

TEACHER: I want to know how many doors and windows are in my house. Let's practice in our classroom. How many doors do you see?

JOSE: I see the front door and the back door. Two doors.

JAMESHIA: Are there doors on the cupboards? We can count those as doors, too.

TEACHER: Yes, we need to decide what we mean by doors. Who has an idea about what we mean by doors?

NANCY: Doors open and close to let people and things in and out.

DARREN: We should count the cupboard doors and room doors.

TEACHER: So, if we count the room doors only, we will get one number, but if we count the room doors and the cupboard doors, we will get another number. How many windows do we have in our room?

JASMINE: If I count the big windows, we have 10, but if I count all of the small pieces, we have 60.

TEACHER: Tonight, I would like you all to count the number of doors and windows in your house. You may have more than one way of counting them.

Vignette 5, Grade 6
Integration: Math/Oral Language

In this classroom, the teacher wanted to involve the students in decision making. To help support the decision-making process, the teacher had students transform actual measurements into a symbolic format. (The students understand the concept of proportion.)

TEACHER: You have gathered information from primary-grade students about what they would like for a new playground. You also searched the Internet for playground equipment. Now it is time for your groups to put together proposals and plans. Other than what the students like, what other criteria do we need to consider?

HOWARD: We need to understand how much the equipment costs.

TEACHER: Yes. Is there anything else?

RACHEL: We need to know where the equipment will be placed on the field and if it will all fit into the space we have.

TEACHER: Yes. Who has an idea about the next steps we can take?

LITA: We can go out onto the field and measure and lay out where we think different games and equipment can go.

TEACHER: That is a good idea, but we may not be able to spend all of our time out there. Does anyone have an idea about how we can work on this problem in our classroom?

JEMMA: We can draw a design on paper. It will have to be smaller than the actual playground or it would not fit in our classroom. We couldn't move around.

TEACHER: You are thinking like a mathematician. You are deciding to use ratios and proportions. Let's see what happens with your designs.

QUESTIONING IN SCIENCE

Moyer, Hackett, and Everett (2007) suggest that teachers ask students carefully crafted questions to elicit explanations of specific phenomena. To avoid asking only factual questions, they recommend that questions be used for the following purposes:

- To assess and challenge students' misconceptions about scientific principles
- To assess students' understanding of new scientific concepts
- To stimulate students to use and apply scientific concepts to other curricular areas and in their everyday lives

Vignette 6, Grade 2
Integration: Science/Math (Measuring)/Oral Language/Writing

In the following second-grade class, the teacher helped the students become more structured and systematic in their inquiry. The students experimented with five different substances: sugar, baking soda, "oobleck" (cornstarch), salt, and flour. The teacher provided clear plastic glasses. Each glass held about 8 ounces (250 mL) of water, which had been cooled to room temperature. Each glass was then placed on a sheet of paper on which was printed the name of the substance to be added. Students worked in small groups of three, each with the oobleck and two other substances.

One student in each group measured ¼ teaspoon (1 mL) of one substance and then sprinkled it into a glass. Another student in the group counted to 30, after which the first student stirred the water gently with a spoon. A third student wrote down observations when the water stopped moving. This process was repeated for all substances, with careful observations noted each time.

The following discussion took place after the above processes had been completed.

TEACHER: What happened when you put the sugar in the water?

TONYA: It disappeared. Quickly.

TEACHER: Why do you think this happened?

TONYA: It mixed with the water.

JARED: It happened every time we added it. Sugar goes away in water.

TEACHER: What about the baking soda? What happened with it?

GREG: It went away in the water every time, too.

TONYA: Ours didn't, not like the sugar.

TEACHER: Okay. What did the rest of you find with the baking soda? Linda? Beth? Nuri? (*Pauses.*)

LINDA: It mixed right up quickly.

BETH: Ours did, too.

NURI: It disappeared faster than the sugar.

TEACHER: Okay, in general, then, we can say that the sugar and the baking soda mixed with the water or dissolved in it. (*Writes* dissolved *on the whiteboard.*) What about the salt? (*Pauses.*) Nuri?

NURI: It went away – it dissolved right away – but the water was all white.

TONYA: Yeah, it never went away, and every time we added more it was whiter.

JARED: Some salt pieces even dropped on the bottom.

BETH: Yes, that happened to ours, too.

TEACHER: So, can anyone make a statement about sugar and baking soda compared to salt?

LINDA: Sugar and soda dissolve better than salt does.

TEACHER: Thumbs up if you agree with Linda's statement. (*Pauses.*) I see you all agree. What happened with the flour? Jared?

JARED: It got all cloudy. The water was all murky. And then it just sank to the bottom.

TEACHER: Murky is a good word! Did anyone observe anything different from that happening?

LINDA: Flour didn't mix at all with the water.

BETH: It mixed up, but it didn't go away. It didn't dissolve.

TEACHER: Any statements you care to make about the flour compared to the baking soda, salt, or sugar? (*Pauses.*) Tonya? Jared? Linda?

TONYA: The flour was slower mixing up than the salt, and sugar is fastest.

LINDA: Baking soda dissolves as good as sugar.

JARED: And salt is better than flour, but doesn't really dissolve.

TEACHER: Good observations! Now, what was happening with the oobleck?

LINDA: The oobleck never went away, either. The oobleck doesn't dissolve, just like the flour doesn't dissolve.

TONYA: But it did faster with ours than the flour.

TEACHER: How many of you found that the oobleck was different from the flour? (*Pauses.*)

NURI: It went like this: Sugar and baking soda dissolved totally, salt mixed up a little bit, but made the water cloudy and didn't dissolve, and then the flour and the oobleck kept getting glumpier and glumpier in the water.

Vignette 7, Grade 1
Integration: Science/Ecology/Reading/Social Studies

This first-grade social studies teacher began her lesson about trees with a K-W-L (Ogle 1986). The questions in each category resulted in the following responses from the students, which the teacher listed on the whiteboard:

TEACHER: What do you know about trees?

Students' Answers:
- They have leaves.
- Some shed their leaves, some don't.
- They give us shade.
- Animals live in them.
- We get wood from them.
- You can climb them.
- They give us fruit.
- Some have flowers.

TEACHER: What would you like to know about trees?

Students' Answers:

- How long do they live?
- How can we protect them?
- How can we take care of them?
- If you cut them down, do they grow back?
- What kills trees?

At this point, the teacher read the students the book, *Someday a Tree*, by Eve Bunting, a story about a little girl who tells why an oak tree is important to her. This particular tree is dying, and even the townspeople cannot save it. The girl plants an acorn, hoping it will grow into a grand oak.

After listening to the story, the students revisited their questions (see above).

TEACHER: What did we learn about trees?

Students' Answers:

- Some trees live as long as people do.
- Trees do not grow back after they are cut down.
- Trees can't be protected like animals are, but by planting trees like the girl did, you make sure there are always new ones around.

TEACHER: How has your thinking or feeling changed after listening to this story?

Students' Answers:

- I never really thought about trees before. I just felt like they would always be there.
- I didn't know trees died like people.
- I didn't know trees are alive.
- I know now it takes a long time for a tree to grow.
- I want to plant some trees too.
- I appreciate trees more now.

The class then went on a field trip to a local nursery where the nursery owner showed the students many different kinds of trees and explained which grew naturally in their area, which were drought-resistant, and so on. The nursery owner answered questions the students had about trees, such as, How can we take care of them? and What kills them?

TEACHER (*Back in the classroom.*): Which tree is your favorite and why?

The students' answers were graphed on chart paper. As an assignment, students were asked to collect acorns in their neighborhood. The following week, each student then planted an acorn in the schoolyard with teacher supervision.

Vignette 8, Grade 6
Integration: Science/Ecology/Social Studies/Reading

The teacher began a lesson on the topic of littering by asking the students, What are some things people can do to help the problem of littering? Using Quick Write[2] (Moore, Readence, and Rickelman 1989), students wrote for three minutes.

After sharing their individual responses in small groups, students read Kenneth Lundberg's essay, "My Twenty Foot Swatch," to find out what one young man's solution was to the pervasive problem of littering.

The teacher then put the students in either dyads or triads to share the passage, using summarizing and questioning techniques. One pair, John and David, proceeded with David reading aloud two paragraphs.

JOHN (*Summarizing.*): The guy in the story asks if we have ever felt so frustrated about world problems that we just did nothing or did something to make it worse. Then, he goes on to say he walks across this field every day and notices all the junk that people have thrown on it at soccer games – candy bar wrappers and stuff.

DAVID: Okay, here's my question: If he is so concerned about world problems like pollution, and the environment, and everything, why didn't he do something about all that litter?

JOHN: Maybe it would make him late for wherever he's going. I mean, would you pick up somebody else's garbage? Anyway, I think he will do something about it in the next part. (*Reads next two paragraphs aloud.*)

DAVID (*Summarizing.*): You're right. He does do something about it. First, he's so disgusted that he writes letters to people at the newspaper and suggests a clean-up day. But then he decides to do it himself. He decides that every day he's going to pick up some litter when he walks back and forth across the field.

JOHN: Did he actually write the letter, or was he just thinking about it?

DAVID: Well... (*Reviews the paragraphs.*) Okay, he just was thinking to do that but then he thought it wouldn't work anyway, and it would probably just raise up his blood pressure. (*Reads next two paragraphs aloud.*)

JOHN (*Summarizing.*): He picked up stuff every day, making a game out of it. Finally, one day he found out he was picking stuff up faster than the people were littering. First, he brought all of the garbage home with him. Then, some janitor brought some trash cans at each end of the field.

DAVID: Did the janitor do that to help him out, or was it just a coincidence?

JOHN: It says the maintenance man was a conspirator. I think that means he was helping him out. (*Reads next paragraph.*)

---

2. Quick Write is a strategy whereby students write everything they can think of about a topic for a short period of time.

DAVID (*Summarizing.*): The guy says he's done this now for a couple of years, and the field is not much cleaner, and people are still littering. But he says he likes it, because it has changed *him*. He is happier and more positive, because he's doing something about it.

JOHN: Why wouldn't he still be frustrated if it really isn't changing anything?

DAVID: He just somehow feels he's doing his part. Maybe it will say more about this in the next part. (*Reads next paragraph.*)

JOHN (*Summarizing.*): This guy wants every place he goes to be a little bit better because he was there. Not only cleaning a little litter, but being kind to people and treating everybody he meets as equals.

DAVID: What does this have to do with littering?

JOHN: It's just a piece of all the problems in the world that he was talking about first. He started with littering, but then he realized he could do little stuff about all the world's problems. (*Reads next paragraph.*)

DAVID (*Summarizing.*): He ends by saying that too many people who speak loudly about world problems care more about being right than really doing anything about them. People should not try to do more than they can do, but they should just do something.

JOHN: Can't you be right and do stuff at the same time? I mean, he was right. How can you be too concerned about being right?

DAVID: I think he means they weren't doing enough; they were just talking about it too much. He would think, don't write a letter about it, get out there and do something about the problem yourself!

After the groups had finished reading the passage, the teacher asked the students to brainstorm the following questions as a whole class:

- What are some local litter or recycling problems that you know about?
- What are some general solutions to this problem?
- What are some individual actions you can take right now?

After much discussion, each student was asked to sign a contract (see figure 7.1) committing to whatever individual action he or she wished.

Vignette 9, Grade 4
Integration: Science/Social Studies

This fourth-grade teacher wanted to give her students an opportunity to get reactions to one another's questions, because peer perceptions often bring additional insight to questioning behavior. To do this, she presented her students with the following situation: You are stranded in a wilderness area in the Rocky Mountains for two weeks. You have a roll of plastic, a canvas, a tea kettle, a flashlight, and some dried fruit.

The teacher explained their chance of survival would depend on specific courses of action determined by the questions they raised and the answers they

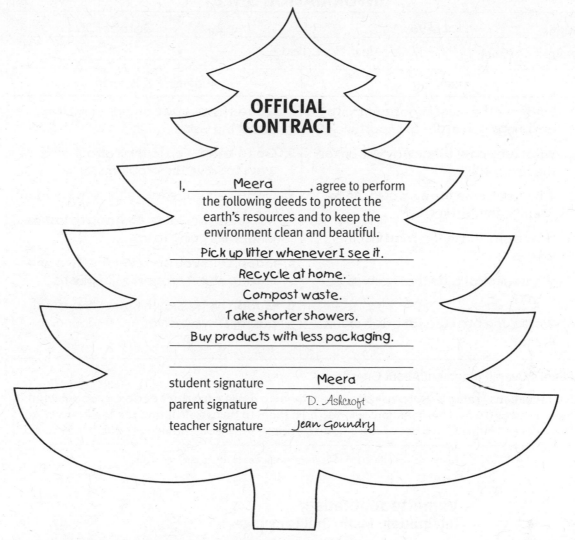

OFFICIAL CONTRACT

I, _____Meera_____, agree to perform the following deeds to protect the earth's resources and to keep the environment clean and beautiful.

Pick up litter whenever I see it.

Recycle at home.

Compost waste.

Take shorter showers.

Buy products with less packaging.

student signature _____Meera_____

parent signature _____D. Ashcroft_____

teacher signature _____Jean Goundry_____

Figure 7.1 Each student can complete and sign an Official Contract.

See BLM 12 in appendix for reproducible master.

received. The focus was not so much on the results, as on the students' ability to analyze whether or not the questions were or were not productive (adapted from Hunkins 1976).

The teacher divided the class into groups of three or four and asked a student in each group to write down the group's list of questions. The students were reminded to reflect on why they chose each particular question. Each group was to evaluate the questions of another group to determine if the questions were productive.

Each panel received an information sheet to record its questions and its judgments (see figure 7.2).

INFORMATION SHEET

Name: **Trevor** Date: **October 25**

Names on Panel: **Katie, Alexi, Marc, Jade**

Question	Judgment & Reason
1. What are the most important things I am bringing, in order of importance?	1. Good. Makes you compare and think about the value.
2. What are some other ways I can use the tea kettle?	2. Good. Leads you to think about other ways to solve the problems.
3. What are some tools I could use to change the tea kettle?	3. Good. Lets you explore the environment.
4. How can I make the food last the longest?	4. Not great, because it's going to last as long as it's going to last.
5. What will plastic do that canvas can't?	5. Good. Let's you compare the two and find out about properties of plastic.
6. What is the best use for each of the items?	6. Good. This gets at the most important part of staying alive.

Panel's Overall Judgment About Questions

The questions Trevor's group asked will help them to make important decisions about what they need and why. The questions will also help them to be creative and use the items in ways they weren't intended to be, which is good because they won't have everything they need.

See BLM 13 in appendix for reproducible master.

Figure 7.2 The Information Sheet is a useful way to record peer reactions.

Vignette 10, Grade 5
Integration: Math/Oral Language

The teacher wanted students to apply their knowledge from various social studies lessons to a real-world problem.

TEACHER: We have read about outer space exploration, but we have not explored how we might use "inner space" – specifically, our oceans. Could we have cities under the sea? What might they look like? What knowledge do we have about science that would help us?

GERALD: Everyone needs to eat. We need to think about biology and how people would meet their basic needs of food, clothing, and shelter.

ASHLEIGH: People would need sources of energy, too. We need to think about physics to know how they would generate energy and use energy.

TEACHER: Let's form small groups, and have each group make proposals about a possible "city under the sea." As you design and make suggestions, make sure you are thinking about all of the areas of science studies we have considered this year. You may want each member of your group to take on the lens of one type of scientist.

QUESTIONING IN SOCIAL STUDIES

There is no clear consensus among educators about what social studies in the elementary school ought to be. The emphases vary, according to the particular proponent, among thinking, knowledge, and good citizenship. We believe that knowledge and good citizenship can be obtained best through an integrated curriculum that addresses a variety of content – historical and current issues – while stimulating the cognitive and affective processes of critical thinking. This can best occur through effective questioning modeled by teachers and assimilated by students, as in the following examples.

Vignette 11, Grade 3
Integration: Social Studies/Science/Art

Activities that require critical thinking often involve careful observation and inference, analyzing information in order to draw proper conclusions. The teacher in this example used a mini-inquiry to develop students' capabilities in these areas.

The teacher selected a brief excerpt from the Disney film *Walkabout* (set in the Australian interior), for the students to observe and analyze. Because they were beginning a study of deserts, she used this clip to show key aspects of desert life. The students viewed the clip before having any discussion. They were then asked to draw a rough sketch of some aspect of desert life that stood out for them. When this was completed, the students shared their drawings in pairs, explaining the meaning of each part of their sketch to their partner.

Next, the teacher divided the class into small cooperative groups and gave each group a handout with a list of questions to be answered through group consensus. Here are the questions and a sample of group responses:

QUESTION: What are the main characteristics of this desert?

ANSWER: It is hot and dry. There aren't any trees or flowers. Not much lives in the desert. It's cold at night.

QUESTION: What is the name of the native people who live there?

ANSWER: Aborigines.

QUESTION: Where in the world is this desert located?

ANSWER: In the middle of Australia. Far away from us.

QUESTION: What shelter do the people who live there use?

ANSWER: They have houses like us, but not as nice. Little shacks. Some live in caves.

QUESTION: What is their work?

ANSWER: Some are guides. Some are hunters. Some raise animals.

QUESTION: What are the most important things in their lives?

ANSWER: Finding enough food. Having a happy life. Probably just like us – raising families, being safe, staying cool.

QUESTION: How are these people the same as we are?

ANSWER: They feel love and hate. They can be happy or sad. They are trying to get by in life. They are humans. They care about other people and their families. They like to laugh and have fun.

QUESTION: How are these people different from us?

ANSWER: They don't wear as many clothes. They don't go shopping. Their lives are much harder. They work harder. They speak a different language. They look different.

QUESTION: What are some things we have that they could really use?

ANSWER: Television. An air conditioner. A freezer. Ice cream. Ice cubes. A swimming pool. Irrigation.

QUESTION: What question would you like to ask these people?

ANSWER: How do you like your life? What do you want to be when you grow up? What do you do for fun? Do you ever want to run away? Do you wish you lived in North America? Do you ever wish you could see snow?

Notice that the questions vary across the taxonomy: The first are lower level and then they become more critical and open-ended. After the students gave their preliminary answers to the questions, the teacher showed them the clip again, encouraging the groups to rethink and revise their answers as necessary. Then, the groups shared their answers, discussing differences in responses and revisiting the film clip to settle arguments or clarify points. For example, many of the responses to the question, What are some things we have that they could really use? require electricity, which the people in the film do not have. Since these students had never thought about a culture not having electricity, they learned something important about their own perceptions. Similarly, one group assumed that these desert people would all love to live in the United States or Canada. Other groups challenged this assumption and pointed to instances in the film clip where they seemed content with their lives as they were.

Vignette 12, Grade 1
Integration: Citizenship/Role-Playing/Oral Language

During recess, Nelson allegedly pushed Armando to the ground when it was his turn to be up in kickball. Lydia, who saw the whole event, reported it to her teacher. When the teacher asked Nelson what happened during the game, Nelson did not respond. Armando was no longer crying, but he was still upset. Lydia shared that Nelson was probably upset because he had not been allowed to have a turn.

The teacher quickly decided that role-playing was the vehicle through which this unfortunate scenario might be transformed into an authentic social studies/oral language lesson – not just for the two boys involved, but for the entire class. The critical-thinking activity helped the students consider the variety of alternative solutions that are available for solving conflict.

The teacher guided her students through the following steps:

1. She had a neutral observer, Lydia, give her version of what had occurred during the game.

2. She selected two students, also neutral, to play the roles of the two children involved.

3. She asked the two actors to take a few minutes to prepare a skit of the incident, exactly as Lydia said it had happened.

4. While the actors prepared, the teacher asked the other students to keep in mind the following questions as they watched the skit:

   • What are the actors doing and saying?

   • How is each feeling?

   • How would you feel if you were either of the people involved in the incident?

   • What are some other ways this problem could be handled?

5. The teacher reiterated the last question, asking each student to think of one other way the problem could be handled.

6. Each student presented his or her version of the altercation.

7. The audience shared several ideas about other ways the problem might have been handled. The debriefing discussion (excerpted) follows.

TEACHER: What are some other ways that this problem could have been solved? Kristen, Jill, and Craig?

KRISTEN: You could have sent Nelson to the office.

TEACHER: That is true; I could have, but then I would have been taking care of their problem. Can you think of a way they might have solved it themselves?

KRISTEN: Well, Nelson could have come to you and told you that he wasn't getting any turns.

JILL: Or he just could have said that to Armando.

TEACHER: Yes, those are ways that don't hurt anyone. Craig?

CRAIG: He could have just gone away and done something else if they weren't being nice. He didn't have to push somebody.

TEACHER: Those are all different ways to solve the problem. Does anyone have another idea? Brandon?

BRANDON: He could have taken the ball for a minute and made 'em stop the game and said, "Look, you guys, I'm not getting a turn."

TEACHER (*Smiles and nods.*): Wow! You thought of lots of different ways that this problem can be solved, and no one got pushed down or hurt. Great job!

Vignette 13, Grade 6
Integration: Global Awareness/Math/Writing

By using a simulation of food supplies of the world, the students in this sixth-grade class gained a relative perspective of global population groups and food supplies (adapted from Chapin 2008).

The teacher started off by asking students, How hungry is the hungriest you have ever been? She instructed children to do a Quick Write in response to this question. She then explained, We are going to see how much food people have in different parts of the world. You, as a class, are going to represent all of the people in the world.

The teacher then divided the class into five groups proportionate to the following percentages:

- Asia: 54 percent of the people; 5 percent of the food supply
- Africa: 10 percent of the people; 1 percent of the food supply
- Latin America: 8 percent of the people; 15 percent of the food supply
- Middle East: 2 percent of the people; 5 percent of the food supply
- West (United States, Canada, Western Europe): 26 percent of the people; 74 percent of the food supply

The teacher guided the students to mathematically figure out the proportionate number of people in each of the five groups for their class of 30 students. They figured the following and were assigned to one of the five groups:

- Asia: 16 students
- Africa: 3 students
- Latin America: 2 students
- Middle East: 1 student
- West: 8 students

The teacher had the students sit at the front of the classroom in their groups, roughly in proportion to their geographical location as they perceived it on a globe.

Then, the teacher brought out a loaf of bread and explained that it represented all of the food in the world. She helped the students divide the loaf according to the proportions listed above by having them calculate the exact portions each group should have. The bread allotment was then distributed to each group. In their groups, students discussed the following questions:

- How does your group feel about its food supply?
- If your food supply were low, could you ask people in other countries to give you some of their food? Why or why not?
- If your food supply were high, would you consider giving some of your food to countries that need more food? Why or why not?
- Do you think your responses are similar to the responses of people in the real world? In what ways?

Each group shared its ideas with the whole class. Here were some of their insights:

WEST: We liked having so much more than everyone else. We definitely think we should share our food with other countries. But we think people in the real world in the West – us – don't think very much about how hungry other people are. We just assume everybody has as much as we do.

ASIA: We were really mad at first, because we have tons more people than anybody else and not nearly enough food to go around. It's not fair. The West should give us some.

MIDDLE EAST: There are groups who have more people than we do and less to eat and fewer people and more to eat. We're in the middle. We probably have enough, but not enough to give away, but if somebody was starving we would. We don't think the real Middle Eastern people feel this way, but we don't really know.

TEACHER: What do you think you would like other governments to do about your situation if you do not have enough food? Asia and Africa, I would like you to write to another government, and tell them what you have learned. What do you think governments should do if they have more than their share of food? West, Middle East, and Latin America, I'd like you to think about this question, and write to your "own" governments, explaining some ideas you have about how to equalize the world's food supply.

Vignette 14, Grade 5
Integration: Historical and Geographical Knowledge/Oral Language/Writing

History is frequently told from adult and political points of view. In these instances, students have to use data and primary sources by and about adults to extrapolate what children's lives were like. We know, however, that children become more historically connected when they can see themselves within an historical context, as we can see in the example below.

The students in this fifth-grade class were anticipating a living history field trip in a few days. Before the excursion, the teacher had students read *Sarah Morton's Day*. This historical fiction is about a young girl living in Plimoth Plantation in 1627 (Waters 1989). The photographs in the story are of a modern-day girl playing the role of Sarah. However, the information was gleaned from primary source materials. After reading the book, the teacher and students had the following discussion:

GLORIA: It is about what we have to have to live. It is food, clothing, and shelter. I think it also means that we need to be loved and cared for, too.

RAJ: Sarah had a lot of work that she had to do. She spent a lot of her time helping her family meet their basic needs. I wondered if this was a regular day for her. She did not spend very much time on school work, and she has a lesson by herself, without other students around.

ROBERTO: I think it was cold – either fall or winter, because she wore a lot of clothes. Even though there was no snow on the ground and the sun was shining, all of those clothes look as though it is cold.

IVAN: She had some games to play with her friend. Even though they called it marbles, it wasn't a game I have ever heard of.

JEREMY: The weather and seasons will affect the clothing they make and wear and the kinds of food they can grow.

AUDREY: The houses may look different, because they have different materials around them for building structures. If they do not have a lot of wood, their houses may be smaller so they use fewer materials.

TEACHER: We are going to go on a field trip soon to Sutter's Fort. Do you think we might create a book about the day in the life of a child at Sutter's Fort? I would like you to meet in small groups to consider the following questions:

- How will you find out about daily life?
- What will you do if the primary sources we find are written by and about adults?
- Do you have ideas about how people met their basic needs?

During this discussion about the book, students gave back-up information and examples in their responses – without prompting or cuing. Their ability to elaborate on their answers was a direct result of strategies that the teacher had introduced earlier in the year. They had examined what a "good" answer needed to include. Whether the students are answering questions from a book or from a discussion, they have learned to provide reasons, evidence, and examples in their answers.

Related Information

Creativity often involves changing or adapting an idea that someone else has had. Students can use movie-making software or presentation software to show what life was like during in the 1600s. They may decide to include how their lives today compare with the lives of children long ago.

Vignette 15, Grade 2
Integration: Historical Timelines/Geography/Oral Language/Art

The House on Maple Street, by B. Pryor, shows a progression of changes that happen over time on a single geographic (imaginary) location. Writing involves the sequencing of ideas. Sequencing can begin with time by providing scaffolding for understanding the order of ideas. Later, students may segue into more complex ways of sequencing, such as setting priorities. It is also important for youngsters to differentiate between what they observe and how they fill in gaps based on their observations – that is, how they make inferences. This type of activity allows students to identify an order of occurrence and then use that information to create their own timelines of their local community. Notice that the categories reflect the disciplines in the social sciences: history, geography, anthropology, political science, economics, and sociology.

> TEACHER: We are going to read a story about one specific location and how it changes over time. I am giving each of you a graphic organizer that has a timeline at the top. As you listen to the story, write words or draw symbols to help you remember the changes to Maple Street.

The teacher read the story, then initiated the following discussion:

> TEACHER: How did the transportation change over time?

> LIBBY: At first, the people living there depended on themselves or animals. Later on, they used carts with animals, and then machines were invented.

> JACOB: Yes, they had tractors, trucks, and cars. They could move a lot faster with machines.

> TEACHER: How did the landscape change?

> CAROL: The first people left everything almost the same. They hunted animals, and their horses may have made some trails, but, basically, the surroundings stayed the same.

> TEACHER: Was that true for all of the people who visited Maple Street?

> MONTY: No, people who came later changed the land a lot. They took down trees, they made roads, they even changed the river.

> TEACHER: Now, I want you to fill in the handout (see figure 7.3) by recording what you actually observed in the book.

After the discussion, students took several minutes to complete the graphic organizer (the organizer may be a student copy or a large class-size copy).

> TEACHER (*After a several minutes.*): How did you know what to fill in at the top of the graphic organizer?

> RILEY: We could see all of the changes either by the pictures in the book or the words in the story.

> TEACHER: Could you use what you observed in the book to answer the sections at the bottom of the graphic organizer?

> TYLER: No, we had to guess. We could see the houses and what they were made from. We could guess about the food they ate. For instance, the Native Americans had skins on their tents. I think they hunted animals and used the skins for the tents and ate the meat.

> TEACHER: Yes, you could answer the top section by looking at the pictures and remembering what I read to you. You could directly observe all of the information you needed. For the bottom part of the handout, however, you had to "read between the lines" – look for hints – to decide about food, values, and roles. This is because you had only bits of information. For example, there are a few hints about food but you had to infer – make guesses about – from looking at the pictures what different groups of people may have eaten.

Extension

This strategy can be extended to apply to local histories. For example:

> TEACHER: Let's think about the land right here in our neighborhood. Who first lived on this land? Then, who followed?

Teachers can use the graphic organizer below (see figure 7.3) as a basis for creating a handout relevant to their own community.

	HOUSE ON MAPLE STREET						
	How has history shaped and influenced the present?						
	1694 ---> ---> ---> ---> ---> ---> ---> ---> ---> --->						**NOW**
Observations — Who:	animals	Native American		wagon train	settlers	houses	city
Landscape:							
Basic Needs: • Shelter							
• Clothing							
Transportation:							
Inferences/Conclusions — Basic Needs: • Food							
Values:							
Roles: • Male							
• Female							
• Children							
Rules & Organization:							
Economic Basis:							
Leisure:							

Figure 7.3 Students used this chart to help them organize information from *The House on Maple Street*.

QUESTIONING IN ART AND MUSIC

The arts seem to be integrally entwined with the need of children to make sense of themselves and their world through symbols. Whereas language is linear and the arts are nonlinear, they are both branches of the same root and can be considered alternative avenues for constructing and conveying meaning. Gardner (1982, 5) suggests that through language and the arts the human mind creates, revises, transforms, and "recreates wholly fresh products, systems, and even worlds of meaning." Because both art and music have the power to help children think critically and creatively, you need to be aware of how appropriate questioning strategies can help construct meaning in this broad domain as well.

Vignette 16, Grade 6
Integration: Art/Social Studies/Writing

This sixth-grade class was studying life in ancient Egypt. They were going to make designs on Egyptian urns made of potter's clay, as they had studied in their textbook. Rather than the teacher telling the students about all the proper techniques for making designs on clay, she told students they could experiment with the materials to discover for themselves how to make effective ancient Egyptian pottery designs. Figure 7.4 shows how one student used a Questioning Sheet to find this out.

QUESTIONING SHEET

Name: _____Petra_____ Date: ___April 7_____

Project: _____Making Ancient Egyptian pottery designs_____

Questions I Raised:

What kind of design do I want to make? Do I want it to look like ones in the book or do I want to make something really original? What materials will I need? How long do I have to do this assignment?

Questions to Which I Responded:

To start off, I answered the first three questions. I sketched an original design and found the clay and the sculpture tool I would use. Then I asked the teacher and he said we have a week to finish our urns.

My Reactions to the Questions I Asked:

My questions helped me get started by seeing the big picture of what I have to do. They helped me get going.

Other Questions I Raised As I Worked:

As I was working, I wondered how deep I should carve the design. Will too much design make it look bad or too little make it look boring? What is it about those Egyptian figures and symbols that make them look Egyptian? I want mine to look realistic.

My Responses:

I had to answer all those questions. I liked the effect when I carved deep, but it got too messy if I carved too deep. My question about too much or too little design got me to have just the right amount I think. What makes it look Egyptian, I've decided, is the way the people are all angular and sideways, so I did it that way too, or I tried to anyways.

My Reactions to My Questions:

My questions helped me to be clear about what I was doing. I felt free to experiment because I told myself why I was doing things.

Overall Reactions:

I learned a lot this way. I learned about Egyptian urns and pottery, and I also learned about how I feel about it. I'd like to do it again and try it a different way.

Adapted from F. P. Hunkins, 1976 (181–182)

See BLM 14 in appendix for reproducible master.

Figure 7.4 Students can use the Questioning Sheet to make their own discoveries.

Vignette 17, Grade 4
Integration: Art Appreciation/Math/Social Studies

A fourth-grade teacher introduced several famous paintings to her students and talked about each painter, the painter's country of origin, and something about the painter's life. One day, she displayed reproductions of Douglas's *Building More Stately Mansions*, Picasso's *Hand with Flowers*, and Monet's *Water Lilies*. She then asked her students to take a few minutes to really look at the three paintings while thinking about the following questions that she had written on the whiteboard:

- Which painting speaks to you the most? What does it say?
- What aspect of the painting attracts you?
- What in your own life does the painting remind you of?
- What are some places, people, or images that the painting brings to mind?
- What would you change about the painting? Why?
- Write down some words and open-ended phrases that express some of the feelings you have about this painting.

To illustrate how these questions might be answered, the teacher selected the painting that spoke to her the most, and mused aloud what the painting reminded her of in her life, just how it affected her, and even what she would like to change about the painting.

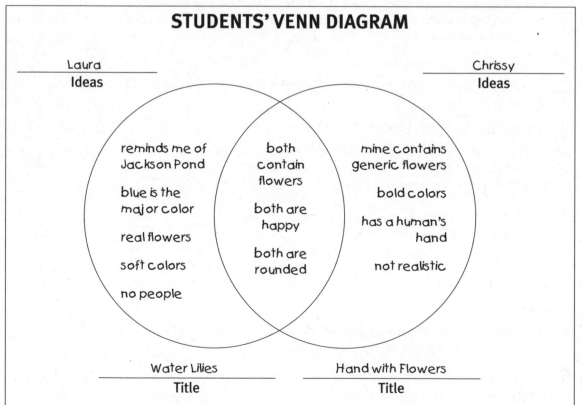

STUDENTS' VENN DIAGRAM

Laura
Ideas

Chrissy
Ideas

reminds me of Jackson Pond

blue is the major color

real flowers

soft colors

no people

both contain flowers

both are happy

both are rounded

mine contains generic flowers

bold colors

has a human's hand

not realistic

Water Lilies
Title

Hand with Flowers
Title

Figure 7.5 A Venn diagram is an effective tool for comparing similarities and differences.

See BLM 15 in appendix for reproducible master.

After students had had time to reflect upon their feelings and reactions to one of the paintings, they were asked to search for a partner who had chosen a painting different from the one they had chosen.

In pairs, the students, using their responses to the questions, made a Venn diagram to graphically illustrate the similarities and differences in the two paintings (see figure 7.5). They then used the Venn diagram as a prop to discuss their feelings about the paintings with the rest of the class.

Vignette 18, Grade 2
Integration: Music/Writing

Students in a grade-two class used a contrast frame (Cudd 1990) to write their reactions to music. The contrast frame provides a literacy scaffold, or temporary structure, for the children to use so that they may begin to record their observations in an expository mode. (A contrast frame can be used by a group or individually.) While such a device is useful in helping students organize their ideas, it is especially helpful for students for whom English is a second language, as they begin to acquire literacy skills.

The teacher selected two pieces of classical music that are very different from each other: Grieg's "Morning," and Grieg's "The Hall of the Mountain King," both from the *Peer Gynt Suite*. After listening to each piece, the teacher asked students to respond to the following questions:

- Of what does this music remind you?
- How does it make you feel?
- What do you see in your mind when you hear this music?
- What does the music make you want to do?

After both pieces had been discussed using the above questions, the teacher asked the students the following questions:

- How are these two pieces of music different from each other?
- How are they the same?
- In what way are they most different from each other?

A contrast frame (see figure 7.6) was then used to summarize the differences between the two pieces of music. It was completed by the teacher, using the responses offered by a small group of students.

> "The Hall of the Mountain King" and "Morning" differ in several ways. First, "The Hall of the Mountain King" is <u>scary</u>, while "Morning" is <u>calm</u>. Second, "The Hall of the Mountain King" is <u>fast</u>, while "Morning" is <u>gentle and slow</u>. Probably the way the two pieces are <u>most</u> different is <u>that "Hall of the Mountain King" is loud and makes me go crazy</u>, while <u>"Morning" is soft and makes me feel all peaceful</u>.

Adapted from Cecil and Lauritzen 1994

Figure 7.6 The teacher used a Contrast Frame to summarize the differences between the two pieces of music.

PART II
Summary

Questioning is one of the essential functions of teaching. Critical and creative questions, well-planned and sequenced, stimulate higher cognitive achievements and make information more meaningful. If these generally accepted assertions are valid, then teachers must achieve a high degree of sensitivity, awareness, and skill in using questioning techniques in the most effective and appropriate manner.

In chapters 3 and 4, we provided you with questioning strategies and activities to stimulate the highest critical- and creative-thinking skills, by inviting the learners to become totally engaged in the process. If learning can be made meaningful and relevant, students will enjoy working at it.

The questioning strategies in these chapters provided you with important tools of the trade. But it is important to remember that they are just that – tools. Each technique must be used appropriately and must be congruent with the objectives that you have for a specific individual, small group, or large class. Finally, it is important that the questioning sessions in classrooms center on worthwhile content. Doing so leads to constructive and joyful experiences in which all students' thoughts and opinions are respected, their interests stimulated, and their minds challenged.

Volumes have been written about what makes children become proficient readers – that is, readers who are able to construct meaning from text. When summarizing these studies, five important strategies emerge that are typical of competent readers and thinkers.

1. They are able to generate questions about text and learning experiences.
2. They are able to summarize.
3. They are able to make predictions.
4. They are able to find important information.
5. They are able to monitor their own understanding of text and learning experiences.

In chapters 5 and 6, we explored strategies that show children how asking their own questions can help them construct meaning from text. Each strategy, additionally, enhanced students' abilities in at least one of the five important skills just listed. Dyad Reading and Schema-General Questions assist students in summarizing; Survey, Question, Read, Recite, and Review (SQ3R), Self-Instruction, and Question Generating show children how to ask appropriate questions; Basal Reader Prediction helps readers learn to predict text; I-Search and Question-Answer Relationships (QARs) aid students, through questioning, to find important information in text and experiences; and both Cognitive Strategy Instruction in Writing (CISW) and Metacognitive Reading offer children insights into how they can more effectively monitor their own understanding as they are reading and writing. Students not only learn from text but also from well-designed experiences. Interviewing/Surveying helps students gather data and then make sense of it. Visual Literacy gives students skills they need to represent their learning in a visual context. No matter where information is obtained, from text or from real experiences, students can use Sequencing as a vehicle for understanding the information they have gathered.

In chapter 7, we looked at how questions can help students understand content and make clear connections across the entire elementary curriculum. Children are natural meaning-makers, always attempting to make sense of their world. Because they are active, constructive learners, they are constantly solving problems, generating and testing hypotheses. Because their hypotheses may be confirmed or disclaimed at any time, risk-taking is inherent in this ever-changing process of learning. Moreover, the hypotheses that are made are usually about some specific topic, a specific domain of knowledge. Hypotheses are rarely content-free. Therefore, what children know – their schema for a specific topic of study and the new knowledge to which teachers guide them – can be the foundation upon which critical questions are formulated.

CONCLUSION

We believe that teaching and questioning are indelibly linked; a notion that is a driving premise of this book. A program of excellent teaching has to, in some way, involve questioning – the teacher's chief means of channeling and stimulating discourse.

The type of teaching we advocate, however, is not congruent with only "know-the-answer-beforehand" questions. You also have to ask questions for which there are no "right" answers. It helps, therefore, to be aware of the various types of questions that exist so that you are able to deliberately form questions appropriate to the context and content of the material, as well as for the ability of your students. By varying the questions, you can then elicit a wide range of responses, thereby developing in your students a broad range of cognitive and affective skills they need for independent and critical thinking. And, since you know neither the answer nor exactly what to expect from your students when asking such questions, you must remain totally vigilant and intellectually involved throughout the entire lesson. This is a most exciting challenge!

When you engage in this type of questioning, you do far more than simply interact with your students – something traditional-questioning strategists often overlook. First, you summarize and sharpen responses and reactions by rephrasing them, thus, spotlighting essential points made by students. Second, you play "discussion traffic cop": you call upon young students who wish to speak and, at the same time, you request that others listen cautiously and comment thoughtfully on the ideas on the floor. Third, by making it clear you are not expecting one "right" answer to the questions you ask, you encourage multiple responses and recitations. Because you do much more than merely question, you often rely on more than just the asking of questions to bring out ideas. Ideas are generated from student responses, and through your own remarks and comments. Therefore, it is not always possible to know ahead of time exactly which question you will ask next. Finally, when you use open-ended questions for which you have no clearly defined answer, you eliminate the pointless game whereby students anxiously attempt to figure out what is in your mind. Instead, you and your students are thrust into roles as "co-inquirers." For the student, this means responsibility, accountability, and above all, profound intellectual stimulation. For you, this means assuming the role of guide to the student as you provide a model of an inquisitive adult exploring new ground.

Provoking students to do the questioning – both of you and of each other – is perhaps the most significant task you face. Clearly, students must learn to question as well as respond if they are to become independent critical thinkers. They learn authentic ways of interacting – out of curiosity, not with conformity or belligerence. To encourage student questioning, you must directly invite student questions, comments, and even, at times, criticisms! Also, you must establish a safe atmosphere in any discourse so that students feel totally free to express themselves without fear of reprisal from you or the other students. It is useful to teach youngsters how to disagree respectfully – that is, how to comment on the ideas, not on the person. You will find the questions students ask arise from an earnest desire to understand both the topic at hand and the position taken by their classmates, rather than as a means to gain your favor.

The most effective technique for encouraging student questioning has been the linchpin of the book; you, the teacher, must establish yourself as a curious, knowledge-seeking role model whom the students yearn to emulate. As such, it is important to not only ask many different kinds of questions, but also to respectfully consider the host of questions generated by your students.

All the teachers you have met in this book represent attributes and attitudes about learning that we have seen in real classrooms in real teachers who have used and continue to use questioning techniques successfully. These teachers have demonstrated a broad spectrum of choices of activities for students to engage in, and they have shown an infectious curiosity and love for learning.

Perhaps the most salient characteristic of the teachers in this book is the way they use their questions to collaborate with their students. In the vignettes in chapter 7, for example, the teachers posed questions for students to consider, supported students' hypotheses about possible solutions for their own problems, facilitated students' own question-raising, and affirmed their struggles with ideas. These teachers realize that knowledge is not just pouring facts or absolute truths into the minds of children as if they were empty vessels. Rather, they are well aware that children construct their own knowledge, their own theories about the world.

There is, of course, no magic formula for teaching. We do believe, however, that teachers must be caring, committed, and ready to ignite the sparks of interest in children through modeling questions and helping children to ask their own questions. The purpose of this book has been to help you be that kind of teacher – the kind who makes learning important to the lives of children.

APPENDIX
Blackline Masters

THE KNOWLEDGE CHART

Name:_____ Date:_____

Topic: _____

Knowledge	Questions	New Knowledge	Research	Reactions
What do you know about _____?	What do you want to know about _____?	What did you discover after reading about _____?	What do you still want to know about _____?	How do you now think or feel about _____?

© Portage & Main Press, 2011, *The Art of Inquiry*, ISBN: 978-1-55379-254-3

RESPONSE HEURISTIC

Name:_____ Date:_____

Theme: _____

1. What is important in the book?

2. How does the story make you feel?

3. What experiences have you had that the story reminds you of?

© Portage & Main Press, 2011, *The Art of Inquiry*, ISBN: 978-1-55379-254-3

PROBABLE PASSAGES: POST-READING STAGE

Name:_____ Date:_____

Theme:_____

Revised Probable Passage

The story takes place _____

_____.

_____is a character in the story who

_____

_____.

A problem occurs when _____

_____

_____

_____.

Then _____

_____

_____.

The problem is solved when _____

_____

_____

_____.

The story ends _____

_____

_____

_____.

© Portage & Main Press, 2011, *The Art of Inquiry*, ISBN: 978-1-55379-254-3

THINK ALOUD

Name: _____

Date: _____

Story Title: _____

1. How often did I ask myself what I thought this story or photograph was about?

never   sometimes   often   after every paragraph

2. How often did I see pictures in my mind of what was going on?

never   sometimes   often   after every paragraph

3. How often did what I read remind me of something else that I know about?

never   sometimes   often   after every paragraph

4. How often did I stop to see if I was understanding what was going on in the story or paragraph?

never   sometimes   often   after every paragraph

5. How often did I change what I had originally thought about what was going on in the story or passage?

never   sometimes   often   after every paragraph

SCAMPERing

Name:_____ Date:_____

Theme: _____

To rewrite the story in a new way, select a question, then answer in the space at the bottom (turn the page if you need more room).

1. Substitute:

2. Combine:

3. Adapt:

4. Modify:

5. Magnify:

6. Put to Use:

7. Point of View:

8. Eliminate:

9. Rearrange:

10. Reverse:

Answer: _____

_____

_____

_____

_____

_____

© Portage & Main Press, 2011, *The Art of Inquiry*, ISBN: 978-1-55379-254-3

Dear_____,

My class is studying about_____.

We have some questions that we are asking _____

_____

_____

_____.

We want to know about the _____

_____

_____

_____.

Would you be willing to answer some questions for me on_____

_____

_____?

We can meet at _____

_____

_____.

Sincerely,

_____

© Portage & Main Press, 2011, *The Art of Inquiry*, ISBN: 978-1-55379-254-3

My name: _____

Person interviewed: _____

I know this person because _____

Date and time of interview: _____

Question	Answer

© Portage & Main Press, 2011, *The Art of Inquiry*, ISBN: 978-1-55379-254-3

DID I:

✓						
	Arrange an agreed-upon time and place for the interview?	Share the purpose of the interview?	Ask all of the questions I had planned to ask?	Keep good eye contact and positive body language?	Ask follow-up questions for more detail?	Thank the person I was interviewing for his/her time and information?

© Portage & Main Press, 2011, *The Art of Inquiry*, ISBN: 978-1-55379-254-3

SCHEMA-GENERAL QUESTIONS

Name:_____ Date: _____

Book Title: _____

Using the questions you have learned to ask yourself,
write a summary of the book under the following headings:

The Main Character:

The Goal:

The Problem:

The Resolution:

The Theme:

© Portage & Main Press, 2011, *The Art of Inquiry*, ISBN: 978-1-55379-254-3

I-SEARCH

Name:_____ Date:_____

Question: _____

What do I/we already know?	**Information:**

	Source:	**What the Sources Said:**
How do I/we find the information I/we need?		

What did I/we discover?	

© Portage & Main Press, 2011, *The Art of Inquiry*, ISBN: 978-1-55379-254-3

CSIW

Name:_____ Date: _____

Topic: _____

What is my topic?

Who am I writing for?

What do I already know about this topic?

Where can I get more information about this topic?

What organizational structure should I use?

What are some beginning ideas?

What are some ending ideas?

© Portage & Main Press, 2011, *The Art of Inquiry*, ISBN: 978-1-55379-254-3

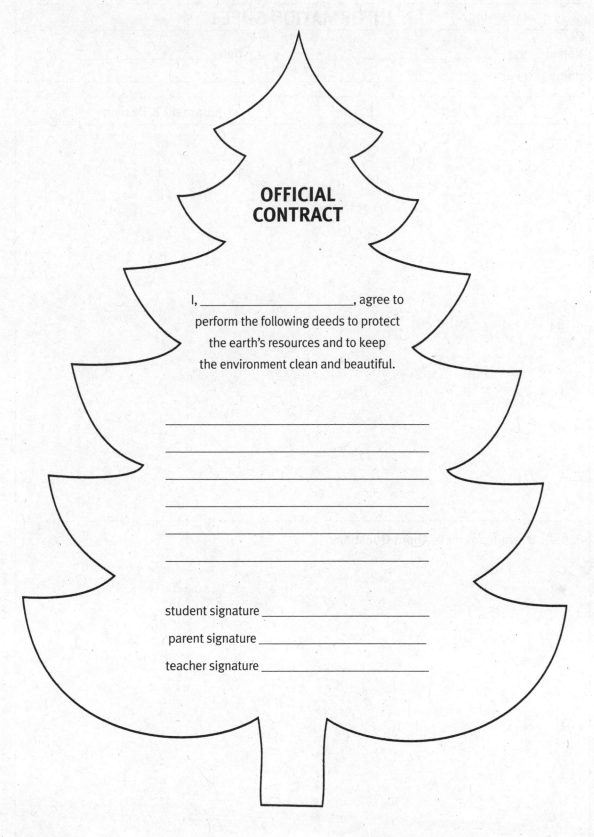

OFFICIAL CONTRACT

I, _____, agree to perform the following deeds to protect the earth's resources and to keep the environment clean and beautiful.

_____
_____
_____
_____
_____
_____

student signature _____

parent signature _____

teacher signature _____

© Portage & Main Press, 2011, *The Art of Inquiry*, ISBN: 978-1-55379-254-3

INFORMATION SHEET

Name:_____ Date:_____

Names on Panel: _____

Question	Judgment & Reason

Panel's Overall Judgment About Questions

© Portage & Main Press, 2011, *The Art of Inquiry*, ISBN: 978-1-55379-254-3

QUESTIONING SHEET

Name:_____ Date: _____

Project: _____

Questions I Raised:

Questions to Which I Responded:

My Reactions to the Questions I Asked:

Other Questions I Raised As I Worked:

My Responses:

My Reactions to My Questions:

Overall Reactions:

Adapted from F. P. Hunkins, 1976 (181–182)   © Portage & Main Press, 2011, *The Art of Inquiry*, ISBN: 978-1-55379-254-3

STUDENTS' VENN DIAGRAM

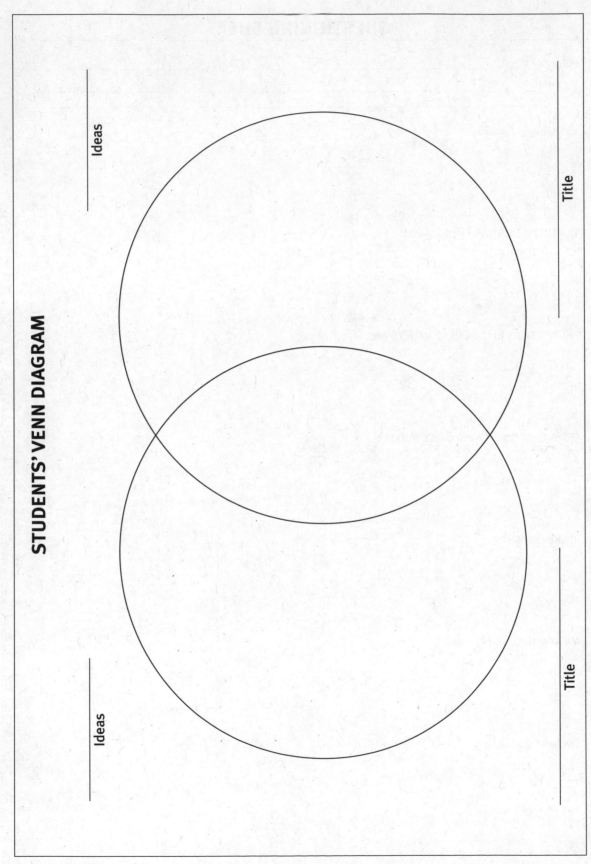

Ideas

Title

Ideas

Title

© Portage & Main Press, 2011, *The Art of Inquiry*, ISBN: 978-1-55379-254-3

REFERENCES

Angletti, S. R. "Encouraging Students to Think About What They Read." *The Reading Teacher* 45 (1991): 288–296.

Armbruster, B. "Content Area Reading Instruction." A presentation given at the Conference on Reading Research, CORR, Las Vegas, NV, 1991.

Ashton-Warner, S. *Spearpoint.* New York: Vintage, 1974.

Au, K. "Using the Experience-Text-Relationship Method with Minority Children." *The Reading Teacher* 32 (1979): 478–79.

Baker, L., and A. L. Brown. "Metacognitive Skills and Reading." In *Handbook of Reading Research,* 353–394. Edited by P. D. Pearson. New York: Longman, 1984.

Balajthy, E. "The Relationship of Training of Self-Generated Questioning with Passage Difficulty and Immediate and Delayed Retention." Paper presented at the American Educational Research Association, Montreal, PQ, 1983.

Barell, J. *Developing More Curious Minds.* Alexandria, VA: ASCD, 2003.

Beyer, B. K. "What Research Says About Teaching Thinking Skills." In *Developing Minds: A Resource Book for Teaching Thinking,* 275–282. Third edition. Edited by A. L. Costa. Alexandria, VA: ASCD, 2001.

Bianchini, J. A. "Mary Budd Rowe: A Storyteller of Science." *Cultural Studies in Science Education* 3, No. 4 (2008): 799–810.

Bird, L. "Reading Comprehension Redefined Through Literature Study: Creating Worlds from the Printed Page." *California Reader* 21 (1988): 9–14.

Blanchard, M., S. Southerland, and E. Grandger. "No Silver Bullet for Inquiry: Making Sense of Teacher Change Following an Inquiry-Based Research Experience for Teachers." *Wiley InterScience* (hppt://www.interscience.wiley.com), 2008.

Blank, M., and D. Allen. "Understanding 'Why': Its Significance in Early Intelligence." In *Origins of Intelligence,* 259–278. Edited by M. Lewis. New York: Plenum, 1976.

Bleich, D. *Subjective Criticism*. Baltimore, MD: Johns Hopkins University Press, 1978.

Bloom, B. S. (ed.) *Taxonomy of Educational Objectives*. White Plains, NY: Longman, 1984.

Bromley, K. D. *Language Arts: Exploring Connections*. Second edition. Boston: Allyn and Bacon, 1992.

Buckley, M. H. "When Teachers Decide to Integrate the Language Arts." *Language Arts* 63 (1986): 369–377.

Cecil, N. L. *The Art of Inquiry: Questioning Strategies for K–6 Classrooms*. Winnipeg, MB: Peguis, 1995.

_____. *Freedom Fighters: Affective Teaching of the Language Arts*. Salem, WI: Sheffield, 1994.

_____. *Teaching to the Heart: Affective Teaching of Literacy*. Salem, WI: Sheffield, 1993.

_____. "Where Have All the Good Questions Gone? Encouraging Creative Expression in Children." In *Literacy in the '90s: Selected Readings in the Language Arts*. Edited by N. L. Cecil. Dubuque, IA: Kendall/Hunt, 1990.

Cecil, N. L., and P. Lauritzen. *Literacy and the Arts for the Integrated Classroom: Alternative Ways of Knowing*. White Plains, NY: Longman, 1994.

Chapin, J. R. *Elementary Social Studies*. Seventh edition. Boston: Pearson, Allyn and Bacon, 2008.

Clyde, J. A., and A. Hicks. "Immersed in Inquiry." *Thinking Now* (online only) *Educational Leadership* Vol. 65 (Summer 2008): Retrieved from http://www.ascd.org

Cooper, J. D. *Literacy: Helping Children Construct Meaning*. Boston: Houghton Mifflin, 1993.

Cornbleth, C. "Student Questioning as a Learning Strategy." *Educational Leadership* 33 (1975): 219–222.

Costa, A. L. (ed.) *Developing Minds: A Resource Book for Teaching Thinking*. Third edition. Alexandria, VA: ASCD, 2001.

Costa, A. L. *The School Is a Home for the Mind*. Palatine, IL: Skylight, 1991.

Costa, A. L. and R. J. Marzano. "Teaching the Language of Thinking." In *Developing Minds: A Resource Book for Teaching Thinking*, 379–383. Third edition. Edited by A. L. Costa. Alexandria, VA: ASCD, 2001.

Cudd, E. "The Paragraph Frame: A Bridge from Narrative to Expository Text." In *Literacy in the '90s: Selected Readings in the Language Arts*. Edited by N. L. Cecil. Dubuque, IA: Kendall/Hunt, 1990.

Davey, B. "Think-Aloud: Modeling the Cognitive Processes of Reading Comprehension." *Journal of Reading* 27 (1983): 44–47.

Davidman, L. *Teaching with a Multicultural Perspective: A Practical Guide*. New York: Longman, 1994.

Eberle, R. F. *Scamper On*. Buffalo, NY: DOK Publishers, 1984.

Edelsky, C. "Living in the Author's World: Analyzing the Author's Craft." *California Reader* 21 (1988): 15–22.

Floyd, W. D. "An Analysis of the Oral Questioning Activity in Selected Colorado Primary Classrooms." Unpublished doctoral dissertation, Colorado State University, 1960.

Franke, M. L., et al. "Teacher Questioning to Elicit Students' Mathematical Thinking in Elementary School Classrooms." *Journal of Teacher Education* Vol. 60 (2009): 380–392.

Freedman, A. "Adapting the I-Search Paper for the Elementary Classroom." In *Practical Ideas for Teaching Writing as a Process*, 114–116. Edited by C. B. Olson. Sacramento: California State Department of Education, 1986.

Gardner, H. *Art, Mind, and Brain: A Cognitive Approach to Creativity*. New York: Basic Books, 1982.

Harvey. S., and A. Goudvis. *Strategies That Work: Teaching Comprehension to Enhance Understanding*. York, ME: Stenhouse, 2000.

Howes, E. V., M. Limm, and I. J. Campos. "Journeys into Inquiry-Based Elementary Science: Literacy Practices, Questioning and Empirical Study. *Science Education* Vol. 93 (July 2008): 189–217.

Hunkins, F. P. *Involving Students in Questioning*. Boston: Allyn and Bacon, 1976.

Hyde, A. A., and M. Bizar. *Thinking in Context: Teaching Cognitive Processes Across the Elementary School Curriculum*. White Plains, NY: Longman, 1989.

Jackson, Y. "Reversing Underachievement in Urban Students: Pedagogy of Confidence." In *Developing Minds: A Resource Book for Teaching Thinking*, 222–228. Third edition. Edited by A. L. Costa. Alexandria, VA: ASCD, 2001.

Jones, J., and S. Leahy. "Developing Strategic Readers." *Science and Children* Vol. 44, No. 3 (November 2006): 30–34.

Joyce, B., and M. Weil. *Models of Teaching*. Seventh edition. Boston: Allyn and Bacon, 2004.

Kestler, J. L. *Questioning Techniques and Tactics*. Boston: Allyn and Bacon, 1992.

Kinniburgh, L. H., and E. L. Shaw Jr. "Using Question-Answer Relationships to Build Reading Comprehension in Science." *Science Activities* Vol. 45, No. 4 (Winter 2009): 19–26.

Konapale, B. C., S. H. Martin, and M. A Martin. "Using a Writing Strategy to Enhance Sixth-Grade Students' Comprehension of Material." *Journal of Reading Behavior* 22 (1990): 19–37.

Langer, J., et al. "Learning to Read in Our Nation's Schools: Instruction and Achievement in 1988 at Grades 4, 8 and 12." In *National Assessment of Educational Progress*. Princeton, NJ: Educational Testing Service, 1990.

Mason, J. M., and K. M. Au. *Reading Instruction for Today*. Glenview, IL: Scott Foresman, 1986.

McNeil, J. D. *Reading Comprehension: New Directions for Classroom Practice*. Glenview, IL: Scott Foresman, 1984.

MERIT, Chapter 2 Project. *Developing Metacognitive Skills*. Philadelphia: School District of Philadelphia, 1986.

Moore, D. W., J. E. Readence, and R. J. Rickelman. *Prereading Activities for Content Area Reading and Learning.* Second edition. Newark, DE: International Reading Association, 1989.

Moyer, R. H., J. K. Hackett, and S. A. Everett. *Teaching Science as Investigations: Modeling Inquiry Through Learning Cycle Lessons.* Upper Saddle River, NJ: Pearson/Merrill/Prentice Hall, 2007.

Nader, R. "An Unreasonable Man." *Independent Lens*, PBS, 2006: http://www.pbs.org/independentlens/unreasonableman/nader.html

Noddings, N. "All Our Students Thinking." *Educational Leadership* Vol. 65, No. 5 (February 2008): 8–13.

Ogle, D. "K-W-L: A Teaching Model that Develops Active Reading of Expository Text." *The Reading Teacher* 39 (1986): 564–570.

Orlich, D. C., et al. *Teaching Strategies: A Guide to Better Instruction.* Lexington, MA: D. C. Heath, 2009.

Ouzts, D. T. "Enhancing the Connection Between Literature and Social Studies." *Social Studies and the Young Learner* Vol. 10, No. 4 (March, April 1998): 26–28.

Palinscar, A. M., and A. L. Brown. "Reciprocal Teaching of Comprehension." *Cognition and Instruction* 1 (1984): 117–175.

Paul, R., and L. Elder. *Critical Thinking: Tools for Taking Charge of Your Learning and Your Life.* Second edition. Upper Saddle River, NJ: Pearson/Prentice Hall, 2006.

Pilonieta, P., and A. L. Medina. "Reciprocal Teaching for the Primary Grades: 'We Can Do It, Too!'" *The Reading Teacher* Vol. 63, No. 2 (October 2009): 121–129.

Presseisen, B. Z. "Thinking Skills: Meanings and Models Revisited." In *Developing Minds: A Resource Book for Teaching Thinking*, 47–53. Third edition. Edited by A. L. Costa. Alexandria, VA: ASCD, 2001.

Pressley, M., J., et al. *Cognitive Strategy Instruction that Really Improves Children's Academic Performance.* Cambridge, MA: Brookline, 1990.

Raphael, T. E. "Question-Answering Strategies for Children." *The Reading Teacher* 36 (1982): 186–190.

Raphael, T. E., and C. S. Englebert. "Writing and Reading: Partners in Constructing Meaning." *The Reading Teacher* 43 (1990): 388–400.

Ritchhart, R., T. Turner, and L. Hadar. "Uncovering Students' Thinking About Thinking Using Concept Maps." *Metacognitive Learning* Vol. 4 (2009): 145–159.

Robinson, F. P. *Effective Study.* Revised edition. New York: Harper & Row, 1961.

Roller, C. "Classroom Interaction Patterns: Reflections of a Stratified Society." *Language Arts* 66 (1989): 492–500.

Rosenshine, B. V., C. Meister, and S. Chapan. "Teaching Students to Generate Questions: A Review of the Intervention Studies." *Review of Educational Research* Vol. 66, No. 2 (1996): 181–221.

Rubin, C. "The Curious Classroom: Answers About Questions." *ASCD Express* Vol. 4, Issue 18 (June 11, 2009).

Sigel, I. E. "The Relationship Between Parental Distancing Strategies and the Child's Cognitive Behavior." In *Families as Learning Environments for Children*, 47–86. Edited by L. Laosa and I. Sigel. New York: Plenum, 1982.

Sigel, I. E., and R. Saunders. "An Inquiry Into Inquiry: Question Asking as an Instructional Model." In *Current Topics in Early Childhood*, Vol. 2, 169–193. Edited by L. Katz. Norwood, NJ: Ablex, 1979.

Singer, H. "Active Comprehension: From Answering to Asking Questions." *The Reading Teacher* 31 (1978): 901–908.

Singer, H., and D. Donlon. "Active Comprehension: Problem-Solving Schema with Question Generation for Comprehension of Complex Short Stories." *Reading Research Quarterly* 17 (1982): 166–187.

Sporer, N., J. R. Brunstein, and U. Kieschke. "Improving Students Reading Comprehension Skills: Effects of Strategy Instruction and Reciprocal Teaching." *Learning and Instruction* Vol. 19 (2009): 272–286.

Sternberg, R. J. *Educational Psychology*. Belmont, CA: Thomson/Wadsworth, 2003.

Swartz, R. J. "Energizing Learning." *Educational Leadership* Vol. 65, No. 15 (February 2008): 26–31.

Taba, H. *Teacher's Handbook for Elementary Social Studies*. Reading, MA: Addison-Wesley Publishing, 1967.

Tierney, R. J., J. E. Readence, and E. K. Dishner. *Reading Strategies and Practices*. Second edition. Boston: Allyn and Bacon, 1985.

Trilling, B., and C. Fadel. *21st Century Skills, Learning for Life in Our Times*. San Francisco, CA: Jossey-Bass, 2009.

Van Hof, J. B. "Using Questioning Strategies to Stimulate Student Learning." *ASCD Express* Vol. 4, Issue 18 (June 11, 2009).

Wendler, D., S. J. Samuels, and V. Moore. "The Comprehension Instruction of Award-Winning Teachers, Teachers with Master's Degrees, and Other Teachers." *Reading Research Quarterly* 24 (1989): 382–401.

Wood, K. D. "Probable Passages: A Writing Strategy." *The Reading Teacher* 37 (1987): 496–499.

Yamamoto, K. *Teaching*. Boston: Houghton Mifflin, 1969.

Yopp, R. H., and H. K. Yopp. *Literature-based Reading Activities*. Boston: Allyn and Bacon, 1992.

RESOURCES CITED

Books

Asbjornsen, P. C. *The Three Billy Goats Gruff*. New York: Harcourt Brace, 1957.

Barrie, J. M. *Peter Pan*. New York: Children's Classics, 1987.

Bawden, N. *The Outside Child*. New York: Puffin, 1994; New York: Lothrop, Shepard Books, 1989.

Birchall, B. *Kahu, the Cautious Kiwi*. Aukland: (A New Zealand Golden Book), 1990.

Brumbeau, J. *The Quiltmaker's Gift*. New York: Orchard Books, 2000.

Bunting, E. *Someday a Tree*. New York: Clarion, 1993.

Gray, L. M. *Miss Tizzy*. New York: Aladdin Picture Books, 1998.

Hutchins, P. *Rosie's Walk*. New York: Macmillan, 1968.

Knight, M. B. *Talking Walls*. Gardiner, ME: Tilbury House, 1992.

Komaiko, L. *Earl's Too Cool for Me*. New York: HarperCollins, 1988.

Lundberg, K. "My Twenty Foot Swatch." In *Saving the Earth*. Edited by C. Franck. Philadelphia: Covenant Press, 1982.

Naden, C. J. *Pegasus the Winged Horse*. Mahwah, NJ: Troll, 1981.

Paterson, K. *Bridge to Terabithia*. New York: HarperTrophy, 1977.

Pryor, B. *The House on Maple Street*. New York: Mulberry Books, 1992.

Rylant, C. *Miss Maggie*. New York: Dutton, 1988.

Saunders, S. *Puss in Boots*. New York: Scholastic, 1989.

Waters, K. *Sarah Morton's Day: A Day in the Life of a Pilgrim Girl*. New York: Scholastic, 1989.

Wilhelm, H. *Bunny Trouble*. New York: Scholastic, 1985.

Williams, J. *The Practical Princess*. New York: Parents' Magazine Press, 1969.

"Young Man with a Mission: Albert Schweitzer." In *Adventures with World Heroes*. Edited by R. L. Whitehead. Chicago: Benefic Press, 1979.

Film

Walkabout. Directed by N. Roeg. Max L. Raab-Si Litvinoff Films, 1971.

Paintings

Monet, C. *Water Lilies* or *Nympheas* (1920–1926).

Picasso, P. *Hand with Flowers* (1958).

Douglas, A. *Building More Stately Mansions* (1944).

Music

Grieg, E. "In the Hall of the Mountain King" and "Morning Mood" from *Peer Gynt Suite*, 1875.

SUGGESTED READING

Anderson, C. W., and E. L. Smith. "Teaching Science." In *Educators' Handbook*, 84–111. Edited by V. Richardson-Koehler. White Plains, NY: Longman, 1987.

Albriton, T. "Honest Questions and the Teaching of English." *English Education* 24 (1992): 91–100.

Armbruster, B. "On Answering Questions (Reading to Learn)." *The Reading Teacher* 45 (1992): 724–725.

_____. "Reading and Questioning in Content Area Lessons." *Journal of Reading Behavior* 23 (1991): 35–39.

Ash, B. H. "Student-made Questions: One Way into a Literacy Text." *English Journal* 81 (1992): 61–64.

Baloche, L., L. Platt, and J. Thomas. "Sprouting Magic Beans: Creative Questioning and Cooperative Learning." *Language Arts* 70 (1993): 264–271.

Barrow, L. H., and P. D. Krantz. "Inquiry, Land Snails and Environmental Factors." *Science Activities* Vol. 41, No. 4 (Winter 2005): 33–36.

Beck, I., and M. G. McKeown. "Developing Questions that Promote Comprehension: The Story Map." *Language Arts* 58 (1981): 913–917.

Benito, Y. M., et al. "The Effect of Instruction in Question-Answer Relationships and Metacognition on Social Studies Comprehension." *Journal of Research in Reading* 16 (1993): 20–29.

Boyd, M., and D. Rubin. "How Contingent Questioning Promotes Extended Student Talk: A Function of Display Questions." *Journal of Literacy Research* Vol. 38, No. 2 (2006): 141–169.

Brady, M. "Cover the Material – or Teach Students to Think?" *Educational Leadership* Vol. 65, No. 5 (February 2008): 64–67.

Burns, C., and D. Myhill. "Interactive or Inactive? A Consideration of the Nature of Interaction in Whole Class Teaching." *Cambridge Journal of Education* Vol. 34, No. 1 (March 2004): 35–49.

Busching B. A., and B. A. Slesinger. "Authentic Questions: What Do They Look Like? Where Do They Lead?" In *Literacy Through Language Arts: Teaching and Learning in Context*, 50–78. Edited by S. Murphy and C. Dudley-Marling. Urbana, IL: National Council of Teachers of Education, 2003.

Camp, W. G. "Improving Your Teaching: Questioning Techniques." *Agricultural Education* 66 (1993): 17–23.

Carlsen, W. S. "Questioning in Classrooms: A Sociolinguistic Perspective." *Review of Educational Research* 61 (1991): 157–178.

Carr, W., and S. Kemmis. *Becoming Critical*. London: The Falmer Press, 1986.

Christenbury, L., and P. P. Kelly. *Questioning: A Critical Path to Critical Thinking*. Urbana, IL: ERIC Clearinghouse on Reading and Communications Skills and the National Council of Teachers of English, 1983. (NIE 400-78-0026)

Clarke, D., and P. Sullivan. "Is a Question the Best Answer?" *Australian Mathematics Teacher* 46 (1990): 30–33.

Clegg, A. A. "Classroom Questions." In *The Encyclopedia of Education*, Vol. 2, 183–190. New York: Macmillan, 1971.

Colburn, A. "Introduction to Research." *Science Teacher* Vol. 75, No. 1 (January 2008): 10–12.

Commetras, M. "Analyzing a Critical-Thinking Reading Lesson." *Teaching and Teacher Education* 6 (1990): 201–214.

Daines, D. *Teachers' Oral Questions and Subsequent Verbal Behavior of Teachers and Students*. Provo, UT: Brigham Young University, 1982. (ERIC Document Reproduction Service No. ED 225 979)

Dillon, J. T. "Do Your Questions Promote or Prevent Thinking?" *Learning* 11 (1982): 56–57.

_____. "A Norm Against Student Questions." *The Clearing House* 55 (1981): 135–139.

_____. "To Question or Not to Question During Discussions." *Journal of Teacher Education* 32 (1981): 51–55.

Dole, J., et al. "Moving from the Old to the New: Research on Reading Comprehension Instruction." *Review of Educational Research* 61 (1991): 239–264.

Dupuis, M. M. (ed.) *Reading in the Content Areas: Research for Teachers*. Newark, DE: International Reading Association, 1984.

Education Development Center, Inc. *Man: A Course of Study*. Washington DC: Curriculum Development Associate, Inc., 1970.

Ellis, A. *Teaching and Learning Elementary Social Studies*. Ninth edition. Boston: Allyn and Bacon, 2010.

Fishbein, H. D., et al. "Learners' Questions and Comprehension in a Tutorial Setting." *Journal of Educational Psychology* 82 (1990): 163–170.

Fusco, E. "What Was the Question? Rethinking Questioning." *ASCD Express* Vol. 4, Issue 18 (June 11, 2009).

Gangwer, T. *Visual Impact, Visual Teaching, Using Images to Strengthen Learning.* Thousand Oaks: CA: Corwin Press, 2009.

Gardner, H. *Multiple Intelligences: New Horizons in Theory and Practice.* New York: Basic Books, 2006.

Gilbert, S. W. "Systematic Questioning: Taxonomies that Develop Critical Thinking Skills." *Science Teacher* 59 (1992): 41–46.

Hunkins, F. P. *Questioning Strategies and Techniques.* Boston: Allyn and Bacon, 1972.

Jenkins, C., and D. Lawler. "Questioning Strategies in Content Area Reading: One Teacher's Example." *Reading Improvement* 27 (1990): 133–138.

Johnson, B. E. "Concept Question Chain: A Framework for Thinking and Learning About Text." *Reading Horizons* 32 (1992): 263–278.

Johnson, K. M., et al. "Use of Modeling to Enhance Children's Interrogative Strategies." *Journal of School Psychology* 29 (1991): 81–88.

Johnson, N. "Questioning Etiquette." *Gifted Child Today* 13 (1990): 10–11.

Karmos, J. S., et al. "Questioning Techniques for the Classroom." *Illinois Schools Journal* 69 (1990): 20–24.

King, A. "Enhancing Peer Interaction and Learning in the Classroom Through Reciprocal Questioning." *American Educational Research Journal* 27 (1990): 647–687.

Knapczyk, D. "Effects of Modeling on Promoting Generalization of Student Question Asking and Answering." *Learning Disabilities Research and Practice* 6 (1991): 75–82.

Land, M. L. "Teacher Clarity and Cognitive Level of Questions: Effects on Learning." *Journal of Experimental Education* 49 (1980): 48–51.

Leeds, D. "The Art of Asking Questions." *Training and Development* 47 (1993): 57–58, 60–62.

Leggo, C. "The Reader as Problem-Maker: Responding to a Poem with Questions." *English Journal* 80 (1991): 58–60.

Lyons, C. "The Use of Questions in the Teaching of High-Risk Beginning Readers: A Profile of a Developing Reading Recovery Teacher." *Reading and Writing Quarterly: Overcoming Learning Difficulties* 9 (1993): 317–327.

Mansilla, V. B., and H. Gardner. "Disciplining the Mind." *Educational Leadership* Vol. 65, No. 5 (February 2008): 14–19.

Martinello, M. L. "Learning to Question for Inquiry." *Educational Forum* Vol. 62, No. 2 (Winter 1998): 164–171.

Marzano, R. J. "How Classroom Teachers Approach the Teaching of Thinking." *Theory into Practice* 32 (1993): 154–160.

McKenzie, J. *Beyond Technology: Questioning, Research and the Information-Literate School.* Bellington, WA: FNO Press, 2000.

Mills, K. A. "Floating on a Sea of Talk: Reading Comprehension Through Speaking and Listening." *The Reading Teacher* Vol. 63, No. 4 (December 2009): 325–329.

Neilsen, Lorri. *A Stone in My Shoe: Teaching Literacy in Times of Change*. Winnipeg, MB: Peguis, 1994.

Olshansky, B. *The Power of Pictures: Creating Pathways to Literacy Through Art*. San Francisco, CA: Jossey-Bass, 2008.

Olson, J. K. "The Crucial Role of the Teacher." *Science and Children* Vol. 46, No. 2 (October 2008): 45–49.

O'Malley, J. L. "Asking the Right Questions." *Social Studies* 81 (1990): 89–91.

Otto, P. B. "Finding an Answer in Questioning Strategies." *Science and Children* 28 (1991): 44–47.

Parker, M., and J. Hurry. "Teachers' Use of Questioning and Modeling Comprehension Skills in Primary Classrooms." *Educational Review* Vol. 59, No. 3 (August 2007): 299–314.

Proudfit, L. "Questioning in the Elementary Mathematics Classroom." *School Science and Mathematics* 92 (1992): 133–135.

Riley, J. "The Answer to the Question Is to Listen to the Answer: An Evaluation of Teacher-Student Interaction During Discussions Preparatory to Reading." *Reading World* 22 (1982): 26–33.

Ring, A. "Effects of Training in Strategic Questioning on Children's Problem-Solving Performance." *Journal of Educational Psychology* 83 (1991): 307–317.

Rogers, D. L. "Are Questions the Answer?" *Dimensions* 19 (1990): 3–5.

Ryder, R. J. "The Directed Questioning Activity for Subject Matter Text." *Journal of Reading* 34 (1991): 606–612.

Shiang, C., and E. McDaniel. "Examining the Effects of Questioning on Thinking Processes with a Computer-Based Exercise." *Journal of Educational Computing Research* 7 (1991): 203–217.

Stafford, T. "Teaching Students to Form Effective Questions." *Knowledge Quest* Vol. 38, No. 1 (September/October 2009): 48–55.

Sternberg, R. J. "Answering Questions and Questioning Answers: Guiding Children to Intellectual Excellence." *Phi Delta Kappan* 76 (1994): 136–138.

Theirs, N. "Web Wonders/Teaching for Meaning." *Educational Leadership* Vol. 82, No. 1 (September 2004): 96.

Therrien, W. J., K. Wickstrom, and K. Jones. "Effect of a Combined Repeated Reading and Question Generation Intervention on Reading Achievement." *Learning Disabilities Research & Practice* Vol. 21, Issue 2 (May 2006): 89–97.

Thomas, B. B. "How Can We Use What We Know About Questioning Skills to Develop Literate Thinkers?" *Reading Horizons* 33 (1992): 19–30.

Thomas, D. K. "Why Questions and Why Answers: Patterns and Purposes." *Language Arts* 65 (1988): 552–556.

Tishman, S. "The Object of Their Attention." *Educational Leadership* Vol. 65, No. 5 (February 2008): 44–46.

Tomlinson, C. A. *The Differentiated Classroom: Responding to the Needs of All Learners*. Alexandria, VA: ASCD, 1999.

Tompkins, G. E.. *Teaching Literacy: Balancing Process and Product*. Fifth edition. Upper Saddle River, NJ: Pearson/Merrill/Prentice Hall, 2006.

_____. *Literacy for the 21st Century: A Balanced Approach*. Upper Saddle River, NJ: Prentice Hall, 2006.

Topping, D., and R. McManus. *Real Reading and Real Writing: Content-Area Strategies*. Portsmouth, NH: Heinemann, 2002.

Treffinger, D. J. "Preparing Creative and Critical Thinkers." *Thinking Skills Now* (online only) Vol. 65 (Summer 2008). Retrieved from http://www.ascd.org on 11/23/09.

Van der Meij, H. "What's the Title? A Case of Study of Questioning in Reading." *Journal of Research in Reading* 16 (1993): 46–56.

Wasserman, S. "Teaching Strategies: The Art of the Question." *Childhood Education* 67 (1991): 257–259.

Wiggens, G., and J. McTighe. *Understanding by Design*. Alexandria, VA: ASCD, 1998.

Wimer, J. W., et al. "Higher Order Teacher Questioning of Boys and Girls in Elementary Mathematics Classrooms." *Journal of Educational Research* Vol. 95, No. 2 (November/December 2001): 84–91.

Wing, L. A. "The Interesting Questions Approach to Learning." *Childhood Education* 69 (1992): 78–81.

Young, T. A., and D. Daines. "Students' Predictive Questions and Teachers' Prequestions About Expository Text in Grades K–5." *Reading Psychology* 13 (1992): 291–308.